JAEPL, Vol. 29, 2024

JAEPL

I0154340

The Assembly for Expanded Perspectives on Learning (AEPL), an official assembly of the National Council of Teachers of English, is open to all those interested in extending the frontiers of teaching and learning beyond the traditional disciplines and methodologies.

The purposes of AEPL are to provide a common ground for theorists, researchers, and practitioners to explore innovative ideas; to participate in relevant programs and projects; to integrate these efforts with others in related disciplines; to keep abreast of activities along these lines of inquiry; and to promote scholarship on and publication of these activities.

The *Journal of the Assembly for Expanded Perspectives on Learning, JAEPL*, also provides a forum to encourage research, theory, and classroom practices involving expanded concepts of language. It contributes to a sense of community in which scholars and educators from pre-school through the university exchange points of view and boundary-pushing approaches to teaching and learning. *JAEPL* is especially interested in helping those teachers who experiment with new strategies for learning to share their practices and confirm their validity through publication in professional journals.

Topics of interest include but are not limited to:

- Aesthetic, emotional & moral intelligences
- Learning archetypes
- Kinesthetic knowledge & body wisdom
- Ethic of care in education
- Creativity & innovation
- Pedagogies of healing
- Holistic learning
- Humanistic & transpersonal psychology
- Environmentalism and post-humanism
- (Meta)Cognition

- Imaging & visual thinking
- Intuition & felt sense theory
- Meditation & pedagogical uses of silence
- Narration as knowledge
- Reflective teaching
- Spirituality
- New applications of writing & rhetoric
- Memory & transference
- Multimodality
- Social justice

Membership in AEPL is $45. Contact Jonathan Marine, AEPL, Membership Chair, email: jmarine@gmu.edu. Membership includes current year's issue of *JAEPL*.

Send submissions, address changes, and single hardcopy requests to Wendy Ryden, Editor, *JAEPL*, email: wendy.ryden@liu.edu. Address letters to the editors and all other editorial correspondence to Wendy Ryden (wendy.ryden@liu.edu).

AEPL website: www.aepl.org
Back issues of *JAEPL*: http://trace.tennessee.edu/jaepl/
Blog: https://aeplblog.wordpress.com/
Visit Facebook at **Assembly for Expanded Perspectives on Learning**
Production of *JAEPL* is managed by Parlor Press, https://parlorpress.com.

Assembly for Expanded Perspectives on Learning

JAEPL is a non-profit journal published yearly by the Assembly for Expanded Perspectives on Learning with support from TRACE at University of Tennessee, Knoxville. Back issues are archived at: http://trace.tennessee.edu/jaepl/.

JAEPL gratefully acknowledges this support as well as that of its manuscript reviewers for their expertise and generosity:

Margaret Cuonzo, Long Island University
W. Keith Duffy, Penn State Schuylkill
Mara Lee Grayson, CSU, Dominguez Hills
Peter Khost, Stonybrook University
Damian Koshnick, Western
    Oregon University

Michelle LaFrance, George Mason University
Donna Strickland, University
    of Missouri-Columbia
Christy I. Wenger, Lake Superior
    State University

JAEPL

The Journal of the Assembly for Expanded Perspectives on Learning

Editor
Wendy Ryden
Long Island University

"Connecting" Editor
Christy Wenger
Shepherd University

Book Review Editor
Curtis Porter
Indiana University of Pennsylvania

(ISSN 1085-4630)

An affiliate of the National Council of Teachers of English
Member of the NCTE Information Exchange Agreement
Member of the Council of Editors of Learned Journals
Indexed with MLA Bibliography
Website: www.aepl.org
Blog: https://aeplblog.wordpress.com/
Visit Facebook at **Assembly for Expanded Perspectives on Learning**
Back issues available open access at: http://trace.tennessee.edu/jaepl/

Volume 29 • 2024

Contents

Essays

Connecting

Books

The Confusion of In-Between

Wendy Ryden

"I noticed that it's humid out," reported a student of mine, "but then there was breeze and it was a little cold, too." He added, "It was confusing."

My student had just been outside trying his hand at recording what long-time AEPL associate Irene Papoulis, in her wonderful new book *The Essays Only You Can Write*, terms "noticings"—those fleeting thoughts and observations we have throughout the day that can be mined and pursued for interesting writing material. Although several students found themselves paying attention to the seasonal change and the Northeast September, I particularly liked this student's admission and phrasing about "confusion." I "noticed" how apt his characterization is of not just the weather. We are living in a time of in-between, I think, and it *is* confusing. The weather was once the quintessential topic we relied on to keep our conversations with others civil and light. But even that has changed. Are we having a not atypical, warm September day, we wonder, or is it the harbinger of the ever-increasing temperature that is drastically affecting all life on this planet, fueling human and nonhuman species migration of flora and fauna, forever altering ancient patterns? Suspicion and concern run deep.

I myself am transitioning from a long academic life of research, teaching, and service into a retirement that I imagine will include a lot of reading and writing, but also a lot more time spent outdoors enjoying, learning about, and caring for the natural world, as well as more cooking, and a lot of discarding and repairing—of possessions and home but also of habits and self. Although it will be an adjustment, I am mostly looking forward to these changes, but I have no doubt there will be bitter-sweet moments and that I will sometimes feel lost, scared—confused.

But this personal example is far more hopeful or, at the least, benign in comparison to many other confusions reigning in tumultuous times. We continue to wonder whether America and the rest of the world will find their better angels and resist the bedazzlement of charismatic authoritarianism and the necrotic pleasure of malice. We continue to wonder what we are becoming and what kind of reality we are creating; whether we will have the knowledge and means to live ethically on this planet with both other people and the more-than human. Many of us do more than wonder and actively try to intervene in what sometimes feel like overwhelming odds. In secondary and higher education, we struggle for the academic freedom—and the courage—to confront censorship and book bans enacted and fomented by bureaucrats, grasping politicians, and useful idiots. Universities continue to twist and manipulate curriculum in their never-ending quests to make their institutions financially viable, ignoring best practices in favor of bottom lines. The promises and threats of AI loom large for us. We are optimistic that this advancing technology will create opportunities for teaching and learning and yet fearful for the radical change it could mean for our profession. Will we recognize ourselves in the transformations that are happening now?

What is education, reading and writing, becoming? The Assembly for Expanded Perspectives on Learning and this journal have an important role to play in answering this question, as this issue attests: the role of assessment, long a bug-a-boo and political hot potato, must not be the domain of governmental box-checking and so-called account-ability but a truly human activity that helps teachers understand their students better; in a writing world transformed by digitalization, illness and physicality remind us of our ever-present bodily selves that confront traditions of disembodied educations; as we take up challenges to work towards justice, we must also expand our perspectives about what resistance might look like and why it takes the forms it does.

We have long taught our students that confusion and its liminality can be genera-tive, a beginning, an opportunity to deepen ourselves if we can take on the hard work of it, see more than tedium and fear and find the beauty and meaning that lies in the difficult and overwhelming. Our challenges show no sign of abating, and we hope they present opportunities as well. I wish us all the best in rising to the occasion and finding our ways into and through.

Work Cited

Papoulis, Irene. *The Essays Only You Can Write*. Broadview Press, 2024.

MOFFETT'S CORNER

Steven Lafer and Jonathan Marine, Editors

In this special edition of Moffett's Corner, Sheridan Blau, former Professor of Practice in the teaching of English at Teachers College, Columbia University interviews the noted composition theorist Sondra Perl in order to solicit her memories of the late James Moffett and his influence on her thinking, teaching, and writing. As long-standing members of the field who knew and worked with Moffett, as former site directors with the National Writing Project, and as AEPL Advisory Board members who have been involved with the assembly since its inception, Blau and Perl are in a unique position to reminisce about Moffett's legacy through their personal and professional experiences with him. This interview also serves as a forthcoming chapter in the edited collection, *The Legacy of James Moffett: His Shaping Influence on Writing Studies, English Education, and the Teaching of English*, slated for publication later this year by the National Council of Teachers of English (NCTE).

JAEPL, Vol. 29, 2024

Remembering James Moffett: An Interview and Dialogue with Sondra Perl

Sheridan Blau with Sondra Perl

Introduction to Sondra Perl

Sondra Perl is Professor Emerita of English at the Graduate Center of the City University of New York, where she directed the Ph.D. specialization in Composition and Rhetoric. She is also a founder (with Richard Sterling and John Brereton) and former Director of the New York City Writing Project, a site of the National Writing Project, at Lehman College, CUNY. In 2006, she founded the Holocaust Educators Network which was modeled on the National Writing Project. In 2015, that project was renamed The Olga Lengyel Institute for Holocaust Studies and Human Rights (www.toli.us), where she now serves as the Senior Director for National Programs in the United States.

As one of the most influential scholars of the first generation of modern composition researchers, Perl produced a series of research studies in the early 80s that helped to uncover and describe the mental and embodied experiences of student and adult writers as they engage in the writing process. She also conducted seminal research on classroom teachers in their teaching of writing, and published that research in 1986 (in collaboration with Nancy Wilson) in their powerfully influential book titled *Through Teachers' Eyes: Portraits of Writing Teachers at Work* (Heinemann: reprinted in 1998), a volume that served as a model for a generation of researchers who sought to provide ethnographic accounts of classroom teachers in their daily work of teaching.

In her teaching and her composition research, Sondra Perl has emphasized the importance of a writer's "felt sense" as the pre-verbal source for the ideas that activate a process of discovery and articulation in language. Her 2004 book, *Felt Sense: Writing with the Body* (Boynton/Cook) remains an authoritative and widely consulted guide for helping writers discover and make available to themselves their own most creative and potentially influential ideas. (For a digital copy of the book and a short video of Perl discussing its history, go to https://compcomm.commons.gc.cuny.edu/feltsense/)

Perl's attention to the non-verbal sources for a writer's ideas was of particular interest to Jim Moffett who often spoke about it to colleagues, although in the interview transcript below, she does not recall speaking with Moffett about that work when she first met and collaborated with him. In the interview here, Perl tells the story of how she and Moffett spent a week working together in the summer of 1979, providing a professional development seminar on the teaching of writing for teachers in the Shoreham-Wading River school district on Long Island, NY. During this summer institute, Sondra participated in workshops led by Moffett, and in this interview, she describes in great detail a few of the methods he employed. Moffett's practices were so engaging and successful, in fact, that Perl adopted them for use in her own classrooms when teaching writing to undergraduates and graduate students at CUNY and in her workshops with teachers in the New York City Writing Project and with other educators across the US and in the

EU. Teachers reading these descriptions of Moffett's teaching are likely to find in them models they too will be inspired to adapt for use in their own writing classrooms, wherever they teach.

The Interview

Sheridan Blau: Let's talk about Jim. As you know, we are collecting essays and other materials by and about Jim for a volume that will introduce a new generation of English teachers to his thinking and influence on the teaching of English.

Sondra Perl: Let's do it. This is a great project honoring a great man.

Sheridan Blau: Can you tell me about how you knew Jim personally and professionally and in what context and during what period of time?

Sondra Perl: You know, ever since you've asked me to do this interview, I've been thinking about my history with Jim. And it begins not so much with Jim himself as with my living at home in New Jersey on leave from college for a semester in the late 60's. I didn't think I was going to be a teacher, but I decided I would enroll at a local college and take a course in teaching. The professor assigned the first edition of Jim's book from 1968. [Shows Student Centered Language Arts: K-13, 1st edition (SCLA)]

Sheridan Blau: I have that book, the same edition!

Sondra Perl: If you had told me then, as an undergraduate, that I would have a role to play in the field of composition and rhetoric, and that I would come to know Jim Moffett, I would not have believed you!

Sheridan Blau: What college did you come home from?

Sondra Perl: I went to Simmons College in Boston. I came home for a semester because my sister was ill, and since I had always taken a lot of credits, I could afford some time off. I'm not even sure what led me to take this course; it was at Montclair State with a young professor, who said, "This guy [Moffett} is going to go places; this is someone you should all read."

Sheridan Blau: Do you remember who the professor was?

Sondra Perl: Nope. But I kept the book. I've looked at what I underlined back then and, not surprisingly, found ideas that still resonate today. But after that course and as my sister was getting well, I put it aside. When, a few years later, I enrolled at NYU to pursue a doctorate in English education, Moffett's work eventually became a part of my background reading. During graduate school, I also began teaching writing at the City University of New York. That is when I understood that the standard textbooks being assigned for basic writing and freshman composition tended to be formulaic and that Moffett's SCLA was so much richer.

Sheridan Blau: In the meantime, at NYU were your professors confirming your earlier sense of the importance of Moffett?

Sondra Perl: They must have been.

Sheridan Blau: Who were you working with?

Sondra Perl: Gordon Pradl and John Mayher.

Sheridan Blau: And you don't remember them emphasizing the contributions of Moffett?

Sondra Perl: We're talking 1970, 1971, 1972 …They were very influenced by Louise Rosenblatt, by transactional ideas of reading, and the London Schools Council with Jimmy Britten and Nancy Martin. Gordon had been an undergraduate at Amherst and was also influenced by Theodore Baird who founded the Amherst school of writing. Although Moffett's work, including *Teaching the Universe of Discourse*, must have been on our reading lists, I don't know that Moffett himself was visibly on the scene yet.

Sheridan Blau: Well, he was, and was already widely influential in California, but not so much, I suppose, in New York. And was Louise still at NYU when you were there?

Sondra Perl: Yes, she interviewed me, but I think I was in the last cohort that she accepted before she retired.

Sheridan Blau: So, you never had a course with her?

Sondra Perl: I never had a course with her, but I did with Mitchell Leaska who was very close to her.

Sheridan Blau: Leaska himself was an important literary scholar who, by the way, wrote about Virginia Woolf, as did Moffett. You know, Moffett wrote his prize-winning senior thesis essay at Harvard on Woolf, specifically on her narrative point of view, which led directly to his interest (which he called his "obsession") with perspective and the thinking of writers in relation to audiences.

Sondra Perl. Fascinating! But strangely, I don't recall anyone talking about Moffett in my early days at NYU. But then I got involved in writing research, and I did a dissertation focused on the composing process. So, I must have read more Moffett in that period. But to talk about when I really got to know him, we have to jump to the National Writing Project. You know, Richard Sterling, John Brereton, and I started the New York City Writing Project in 1978. In 1979 and 80, Richard and I were contracted to bring the writing project model to the Shoreham-Wading River School District, which employed some forward-thinking administrators. They decided to devote a portion of their summer budget to a three-week Writing Project Summer Institute designed exclusively for teachers in their district. They asked if there was anyone we wanted to invite to work with us that first summer, the summer of '79, and we came up with the idea of inviting Jim for a week.

Sheridan Blau: That's terrific.

Sondra Perl: It was fabulous. We had three weeks, and reserved one of those weeks for working with Jim. It also happened that the superintendent of schools for the district was traveling during the week that Jim would be doing the instruction, and he offered us his house so that we could avoid a long commute from Manhattan. So, Jim and I shared the superintendent's house and made the short drive together back and forth to the seminar every single day. At the seminar, Jim demonstrated everything he believed in. He didn't talk to us about good teaching; he embodied the spirit and the work of a good teacher. The teachers and Richard and I sat with him and read and wrote and laughed and shared and did group work, really engaging in all of the amazingly rich and complex activities that Jim understood to be the most powerful and generative way to teach writing.

Sheridan Blau: How terrific.

Sondra Perl: That's how I got to know him well. I also learned that he only used the name "Jim" in public and professional settings but at home he preferred to be called "Prana."

Sheridan Blau: I didn't know that.

Sondra Perl: You didn't know that?

Sheridan Blau: No, I got to know Jim and his wife well in his late years, but I don't think he ever told me that, though now that you say it, I am starting to remember something they may have told me about it.

Sondra Perl: He always referred to himself as "Prana" and Jan, his wife, called herself "Yamuna." I have been thinking about his chosen name because the meaning of "Prana" is "breath." Jim was a practitioner of yoga and meditation, practices which are grounded in breathing. It occurred to me recently that the name he chose for himself is so fitting because in so many ways Jim breathed new life into the field of English studies. In fact, in the 50s and 60s, if writing was taught at all, it was, as Janet Emig often said, both a 'limited and limiting' affair, based on a linear model with strict steps leading to the creation of the five-paragraph essay. In other words, for decades, the teaching of writing was focused on products, not processes, and Prana was one of the scholars in the field who worked to enlarge our understanding of writing and literacy, really breathing new life into the curriculum for so many teachers and for their students.

Sheridan Blau: I am now remembering that I did know about Jan's name, because they used to come to Santa Barbara every summer, so Jim could do a presentation at my Writing Project site, and they always chose to come when they could stay over for her birthday weekend, and I'd spend time with them during the weekend, and he would refer to Jan as Yamuna. But I didn't remember him telling me about his own name, until just now. He told me that he had the name, but didn't ask me to call him by it, and I never did, and never heard Jan do it either. I would expect that he used his Hindu name more

7

in the early years when they were running the Ashram in their house in Berkeley. But by the time you worked with him, were they already living in Mariposa?

Sondra Perl: That's right. I went to Mariposa at one point, and he also stayed with us in Manhattan at one point. But it was working with him, day in and day out in Long Island, and watching the way he worked with teachers that showed me the richness of what he had to offer. The Writing Project, as you well know, has changed the practices of thousands of teachers across the country as it changed my practice, but it was Jim who got me to understand how the methods he developed work in a classroom. I can say more about that, but…

Sheridan Blau: By all means, say more!

Sondra Perl: Well, you mentioned that you would be asking me about what ideas or practices I used that came from Jim and which texts or ideas were most influential for me. And the answer is definitely material in the first edition of *Student-Centered Language Arts: K-13*. Just the idea of adding the "13" shows that he understood that really powerful generative teaching, while it may need to be adjusted for level and cognitive ability, can be based on the same ideas and principles from kindergarten through university. Good practice is good practice.

Sheridan Blau: He was the first to try to cover so many grades with his theory and practice, and maybe the only one who actually did it in a book. I can tell you from experience that publishers don't want to do books that go across too many grade levels.

Sondra Perl: I think that's right. So, what I would really say about Jim, or Prana, is that he was ahead of his time. He understood so well that composing is a meaning-making activity and it happens when we read and when we write and when we listen and when we sing and when we dance, and when we share the sense we make of the sensate world. There are so many ways in which he was far ahead of his time. What he invited us to do that summer in Long Island– which was such a simple, simple thing–was free writing, which he called "spontaneous flow of thoughts." He told us to just go and write. "Don't worry about punctuation," he said. "Don't worry about spelling." We all know the practice from Peter Elbow's work, but Moffett was writing about this in his K-13 methods book, even before Elbow's *Writing Without Teachers* was published. Moffett invited us to move around the school and record the spontaneous flow of our experience and impressions of everything we encountered -- everything we were seeing and hearing and smelling and feeling. And then he suggested that we do this on different days and at different places, or even return to the same place at a different time to see what's different. Moffett then asked us to stop and to label the record of our stream of consciousness according to what was immediate and sensory– like smells and sights and sounds -- and what we were thinking about in memory – images and feelings and thoughts from the past.

Sheridan Blau: I didn't know he did that. That's just brilliant! And he was playing with having people write what he called their "spontaneous flow of thought," before Peter

Elbow introduced freewriting? When did Peter do that? 1973, I think. But Peter says that Macrorie really invented free writing. That must have been 1970 or 71.

Sondra Perl: That's right. I almost forgot. I always credited Ken Macrorie as one of the folks who introduced free writing to get us away from what he called "Engfish." I was introduced to his work at NYU and I loved *Uptaught* (1970). But Moffett describes essentially the same process in his original 1968 methods book for teachers. So, Moffett needs to be acknowledged as the inventor of free writing as a teaching practice. That 1968 volume is filled with amazing classroom practices and ideas and suggestions, many of them, as I said before, ahead of their time. And what I just described to you was only step one. Then there are many other things you can do. You can look at your spontaneous writing for tense to see if you are recording a present experience or a memory, or for whether you're merely recording what's happening, or possibly generalizing, or reflecting, noticing when and why you might have moved into a more or less abstract level of thinking.

What Moffett also introduced to us in Shoreham-Wading River which I have continued to use in almost every writing class I have ever taught, is something he called a "memory chain." I remember being astonished by the writing it generated. If I were planning a sequence for a 15-week writing course, memory chain would usually come somewhere in the third or fourth week. It works like this: You're in a classroom and you look at an object in the room and ask yourself, what does that object remind me of. It will be simpler to grasp if I demonstrate it right now for you. So, I'm going to look at the artwork that is behind me which consists of several different kinds of flowers. I'm going to ask myself: what does the artwork remind me of? And that might take me on a memory chain that leads me into museums and my love of still life paintings. Or I could ask myself what do flowers remind me of? And that would take me into my love of gardens and gardening. So, you start by using an object to generate a memory. You write a little bit of what that memory is: I might describe what it feels like to be on my knees, planting dahlias, wondering if I need fertilizer. But then you don't stay with that memory; instead, you ask: what does that in turn remind me of? The word 'knees' might remind me of the time my partner needed knee surgery and I'd be off jotting down memories of his recovery. In other words, in a memory chain, you use one memory to elicit another... in a chain.

You do this focused free writing for about 15 or 20 minutes, but what is so surprising is that when you start you have no idea where you're going to end up. And every one of the little constellations of memory that emerge could be the kernel for a piece of writing. Moffett wanted writers to start with lots of material not with a blank page, material you can go back to, that you can shape. And how do you shape it? You bring it to a group. So, Moffett also modeled that with us. We wrote our memory chains and then we shared them. We laughed out loud so often! Some people produced memory chains on a single theme; others jumped all over. I remember once this really clever guy wrote about all the shoes in the room. Someone else wrote about Italian food. The memories come from whatever is elicited by the object, and if you choose a different object you'll go in a different direction. And then after sharing these in groups, you select one of the memories and you do more free writing on that.

Sheridan Blau: That's just so terrific. I feel embarrassed that I never knew about this because I never read Moffett's methods text. I've read almost all of his other books, but I thought, "Not that one – that's not for college teachers," though I remember that its title refers to K-13. I'm afraid my snobbishness blocked me from discovering writing activities that could have enriched my teaching and workshops over the past 50 years!

Sondra Perl: To this day, Jim's memory chain and freewriting exercises are among the most reliable, generative, and fun activities I use in writing classes, helping to create the kind of community and relationships that Jim would say need to be part of a writing classroom.

Sheridan Blau: That's another way Jim was ahead of his time – in recognizing that play and a playful attitude need to be part of the experience of composing, partly to free your attention and also to invite creativity. So, all of your writing project teachers knew about this memory chain exercise, because you did it every single summer?

Sondra Perl: Yes. That is a staple of my practice that comes from Jim. And then, that summer he also had us writing dialogues and monologues – all of the different genres he valued. And we did this fast, so it was a lot like free writing: non-stop, pell-mell, conducted in a 'don't worry about it' attitude. At one point I recall writing some dialogue and Jim suddenly said, "Introduce a third voice." And, of course, doing that shifts the direction you are going in.

Sheridan Blau: This is the movement to drama.

Sondra Perl: Exactly, and his notion of drama - that classrooms should be filled with drama -- and also songs and limericks and haikus. Jim broadened the base that was otherwise available for most teachers and teacher educators. And it lent our Writing Project institutes an extra richness in the way we explored a wide range of genres. I have relied on Jim's work ever since, as a practitioner -- as a classroom teacher and teacher educator for forty-five years.

Sheridan Blau: What a wonderful story. I just love it. I feel sort of brokenhearted that I missed working with Jim in the same way.

Sondra Perl: I'm surprised. You never did any of that with him?

Sheridan Blau: Well, maybe he never had enough time with us. When he visited our Writing Project, I always invited him to do whatever he wanted to do or simply tell us about what he was writing at the time. And he usually did that, presenting some new and provocative ideas, typically accompanied by a new chart reflecting his latest theory. Sometimes he would play with some ideas he was still formulating and talk about more general issues in writing, like the importance of writing from plenitude, and the ladder of abstraction. And he once did a meditation with us. But he never had a whole day to lead our writing project. I'm so sorry now that I never thought of it. We would typically have him for a morning presentation for 2 or 2-1/2 hours. I think we saw him too much as a guru, and not enough as a master teacher. Ach! We could have read the guru, but we missed our opportunity to learn from our experience with the master teacher. My fault!

Sondra Perl: Well, speaking of the meditative part, it seemed to me that in *Teaching the Universe of Discourse* and elsewhere in other theoretical pieces, Jim explored Western consciousness until he got to its limits. You know, rational, logical, cognitive stages. There is a way that Western thinking about intellectual development focuses entirely on mental states and cognitive development, and Moffett was perhaps the first in our field to develop a model for intellectual growth and development relevant to the language arts that took into account the connection between the mind and the body. And now are we beginning to see more of that kind of understanding in the field of writing studies.

Sheridan Blau: I agree. And I think Louise (Rosenblatt) was also discovering something similar fairly late in her career, around the same time that Moffett did.

Sondra Perl: That's interesting. I didn't know that.

Sheridan Blau: She wrote an essay in about 1981 called "On the Aesthetic as the Basic Model for the Reading Process," in which she comes to the edge of denying the equality of efferent, and aesthetic, essentially saying that all reading, if it's to be meaningful to the reader, has to be experienced aesthetically, because if you don't get it in the body, as it were, you're not getting it at all.

Sondra Perl: Right. I can see that logic. I thought Moffett had the sense that Western thinking in the end was sort of closed at the top or didn't get beyond consciousness, and what I'm remembering now is how he loved the concept written about by Julian Jaynes of the bicameral mind (1976), and its implications for education. I think what drew Moffett to Eastern thinking was its much more subtle and fluid understanding of the mind in its relation to the body and the idea that there are different levels and states of consciousness. I think Prana was drawn toward yoga and Eastern mystical thought because standard academic Western conceptions of mind didn't satisfy him. Eastern thinking around transcendence and spirituality really spoke to some core part of him.

Sheridan Blau: I'm sure that's right. And I assume that throughout your long and close connection with him he was especially drawn to all the work you were doing with felt sense, and he must have seen your work as closely linked and important to his own deepest interests and seen your research as having much in common with his own ongoing studies. But was Moffett drawn to Gendlin too? It was the philosopher and psychologist, Eugene Gendlin, wasn't it, whose writing introduced you to the concept of Felt Sense.

Sondra Perl: Yes, it was Gendlin who coined that term. You know I knew Moffett best in 1979. I had already worked with Gendlin's notions, publishing "Understanding Composing" in CCC in 1980, but while I'm sure we shared an appreciation of the body-mind connection, I was also shy about all of that as well.

Sheridan Blau: Shy? I remember you did a powerful workshop on Felt Sense for my Writing Project in about 1982.

Sondra Perl: I remember that – in the beautiful location, overlooking the ocean, right? And yes, I did introduce the guided process I developed. But I was always a bit nervous about that, worrying that folks might feel uncomfortable – even though the process is so safe and generative. In any event, I don't recall major conversations with Prana about it. Our ideas are certainly not dissimilar in approach and theory and we share an appreciation of the connectedness between the mind and the body and going into the body to discover what isn't yet in words. Like Moffett, I was also interested in what's prior to words, what surrounds words and the silence that is part of composing that we don't think about so much.

Sheridan Blau: You know, as you say this, I actually am understanding some things about him better. He writes about the importance of meditation and about how writing comes from that. And I have to confess that I was always a little puzzled by that idea, wondering "how?" How does it come?" And what you just said makes it less puzzling. Because meditation puts you in touch with things that are deeper. It puts you in touch with what you know from the body or from intuition, which is really what it means to experience a "felt sense" – something you know or feel, but don't yet know in language.

Sondra Perl: Yes, yes, and then you can use that as a guide and ask, "Is this really what I want to say?" But there is also an important distinction between meditation and felt sense. Gendlin would say that the point of meditation is to get beyond your thoughts, to get beneath your thoughts, to sit, if you can ever get there, with no thought. And that the goal of using felt sense with writing is to generate thought, but from a really centered place. So, Moffett and Gendlin are not writing about exactly the same thing and may have very different ends, but they're certainly connected.

Sheridan Blau: With that distinction, Sondra, I think we must call an end to our meeting which has already extended beyond the time limit I had promised. But it has also produced more discoveries and insights and useful information about Moffett and his teaching practices, and our own experiences with him than I ever would have predicted. So, I thank you for your generosity and your good memory, and your friendship, as well as for your important contributions to the field of writing studies and English education for the past half century, and I'll end this dialogical interview with the hope that we'll find future opportunities for similar conversations.

Sondra Perl: It's been a pleasure, Sheridan. Thank you for a very enjoyable afternoon thinking about the field of writing studies and the many ways in which Jim helped to shape it. He was a kind and caring person and I am grateful to have had this opportunity to reminisce about him and about the exciting early days of the field.

ESSAYS

Indisposed to Write: Teaching a Visceral Poetics

Miriam Atkin

Abstract: This essay begins from the premise that acts of thinking and writing are shaped immanently by corporeal need. Accordingly, my aim is to sketch a vision of composition pedagogy that acknowledges the moves and modulations of the thinking body. The route I take to get there explores four works of critical prose that mobilize form and content toward a radical re-orientation of body-in-space and body-in-writing. These texts—by Eleni Stecopoulos, Robert Kocik, William James, and Eli Clare—are to varying degrees experimental, demonstrating a manner of textual difficulty that signals the visceral difficulty implied in any act of writing. What follows is a work of both institutional critique and disability studies, examining the ways in which illness and bodily discomfort become intimately intertwined with the locales that are most insistent on erasing all traces of them. In invoking the architecture of writing education—both the spatial design of the classroom and its systemic elision of somatic experience—and pointing to alternative forms, I mount a critique that is more imaginative than diagnostic, more creative than critical.

The *classroom* signifies a nearly universal set of defining characteristics: an enclosed space with tables and chairs that provide clear sight lines between students' and teachers' eyes and mouths; a large chalkboard, whiteboard or screen operating as a shared reading surface. These structural elements and the activities they are designed to accommodate adhere to the illusion of a lightning fast and unimpeded circuit between language cognition and spoken or written response. Tables ensure that only the organs and extremities symbolically associated with thinking, listening, speaking, reading and writing see the light, which imagines the inhabitants of the room as living processors, opened outward and fully in step with the exchange that defines the predetermined block of time called class. And yet what the tableau strives to hide is predictably, throbbingly palpable—viscerally familiar to any of us who has ever sat in such a room. What we feel in our knees, chests, intestines or underarms when we can't quite get the meaning of another's utterance; or when all eyes are on us and we don't have the right thing ready to say; or when we're achy, congested, nauseated, overheated, hyperactive, fatigued, depressed or afraid and these states feel egregious because the classroom is for minds, not bodies; all of this plays into the scene of teaching and learning as forcefully as does the desire for new knowledge and intellectual discourse.

This largely unspoken role of the body is as fundamental to criticism and scholarship as it is to the operation of the classroom: all works of critical prose, whether consciously or not, voice the needs of a body in space. The writer coordinating thoughts on paper toward the construction of an argument will always contend with her own physical and emotional hurdles along the way, and they will determine the direction of the writing— either by frustrating it, delaying it, or fueling the vigor with which language is enlisted to mask all traces of corporeal need. Reading and writing, learning and teaching—actions in a system of intellectual input/output that is exclusively human and undeniably physical—must move through the labyrinthine channels of the body regardless of how well those channels are functioning. My purpose here is to bring together examples of a compositional practice that treats the essay as well as the classroom— regardless of discipline or topic—as forms of attention to an unfolding visceral present. Such a practice will necessarily entail consideration of how the structures we inhabit press upon our bodies and our words. My project is a descriptive one, aiming to fill out a detailed picture of what a critical writing practice that attends to one's physical and psychical well-being might look like. With this goal in mind, I close-read the forms of somatic investigation that are undertaken in critical-theoretical texts by Eleni Stecopoulos, Robert Kocik, William James and Eli Clare. Questing for an alternative to the gospel of disembodiedness that is my academic inheritance, I use their texts to sketch out a model of critical writing that is self-attentive and self-actualized. Toward that end, my writing—like that of the thinkers I invoke—takes a scholarly approach to lived experience, treating introspection as a productive critical mode. In doing so, I summon my own history as a teacher and a student, edging toward a reimagination of the composition classroom in its symbolic resonance as well as in its lived reality.

Autoethnography in Real Time[1]

In *Visceral Poetics*, a 2016 collection of essays, Eleni Stecopoulos reveals how illness becomes an interpretive and compositional process. In the following description of her symptoms, she describes a manic obsession with the significance of things, a condition in which all elements of her environment became objects to be read:

> At times I felt exquisite pain over almost my entire body, which seemed impossible. My skin stung to the point where I assigned colors to the degrees of pain, a form of relief through translation.... Like my migratory and proliferating symptoms, I became increasingly disorganized and lost my ability to concentrate on any one task or idea. I had always been digressive, but now every detail had enormous significance; I was ruled by manic attention to synchronicity and a compulsion to connect everything with which I came into contact. At night I could not sleep; my mind's eye zoomed over everything I had read, every conversation, every symptom, every bit of self-mythology with which I was tantalized. The experience felt like mania, yet somehow fascinating and wondrous—at once a disease and the very sign of my power to find the way out of the labyrinth. My mania itself seemed to signify my ability to excavate its origin and decipher its true pattern, eventually triumphing over it and its effects on my body. (Stecopoulos 11)

Visceral Poetics is a meditation on the essay as form, originally composed as a doctoral dissertation which the author undertook during the onset of a chronic illness. It per-

---

1. The subheadings in this essay refer to titles and phrases from Stecopoulos's and Kocik's texts.

forms the sick body's resistance to working within the formulae of academic argumentation, yet it is also a positive project that simultaneously exercises and theorizes the possibility for a prose that attends to the whole body of its author, making use of the body's full range of feeling and motion.

Stecopoulos's writing alternates between different forms of attention, using autobiographical narrative (or autoethnographic, as Stecopoulos terms it), literary scholarship (with an extended focus on the poetics of Antonin Artaud and Paul Metcalf), and polemical engagement with theory (taking up works by Michel de Certeau, Jacques Derrida, Eduard Glissant, Ludwig Wittgenstein and Gilles Deleuze, among others) to compose a self-reflective work of criticism that maintains a constant questioning of what criticism is and how it functions. Her project is framed as a response to the limitations of a US academic environment in which "the authority of literary criticism has typically been predicated on repressing that bodies, not minds, write" (Stecopoulos 59). Her attention is externally focused on the poets and philosophers with whom she feels a kinship, and internally focused on the bodily sensations that attend the writing act, discovering "*a link between language and pain*" (59). She finds pain in the effort to corral thought and feeling in a legible sentence, and disablement in the act of engaging with an intellectual tradition and thus entering a realm in which institutional metrics will be used to judge whether or not she's a deserving inheritor of that tradition. Her text thereby traces its own limitations in harnessing the body's resistance to textuality.

Visceral Poetics implements in a literary critical context the epistemologies engaged by the array of movement practices and healing traditions Stecopoulos sought in order to alleviate her illness. In her exploration of Ayurveda, kinesiology, Thought Field Therapy, electrotherapeutics and a host of other healing modalities—which she approached not as a true believer, but as a suffering person willing to try anything—Stecopoulos learned to exert the range of what her body knows through a willingness to make use of painful and allegedly pathological sensations:

> …(R)ather than robbing people of their bodies, on the contrary, [illness] may be one of the only ways they can actually experience the poetics of their bodies. This can act as a kind of fieldwork, and is often present in such dialogic terms by the alternative healing community: one "slows down" and "listens to the body," for "your body is trying to tell you something." (48)

I appreciate the sacrilege of this, as I know from my own extended battle with sleep medicine practitioners, that conventional wisdom—as a reflection of Western biomedical practice—regards disease and discomfort to be at cross-purposes with the sufferer; anathema rather than intelligent, aberrant rather than endemic. Studies have correlated insomnia with diabetes, heart disease, stroke, dementia and a general decrease in life expectancy, and therefore the medical priority is to fix it, not to understand it. I accepted the logic of this as long as I continued to believe that the fix could work. When I eventually learned that mechanical interventions made the problem worse, not better, I began reading the emergence of my symptoms as plot twists in an ever-unfolding story. Any odd or unpredicted event added new layers to the plot, and I was riveted.

I want to think along with Stecopoulos about how to elaborate a kind of personalized, somatic literacy as the groundwork for critical writing. Interpreting moments of visceral unrest against what I know of "feeling normal," and studying the way my private pains interact with my daily external conditions is the kind of attention that medication will always shut down. And it's the same practice I prohibit if I let a student believe that her way into the work of criticism and composition is excessive or ill-suited. Stecopoulos writes: "Whether body fluids or vocables, disease or phatic gestures—to restore the full body to any aesthetic performance is to restore process" (23). There is much value in attending to what *hurts* about the writing process, and, if teaching with a singular focus on fixing the difficulties, the teacher will encourage an excision of the body from the composition, and thus silence the very means by which writing may remain close to the actualities that language purports to reflect. The struggle to think— which will always boil down to a struggle against the body—has a role in writing just as the presentation of a thesis, evidence, and conclusion does. Writers and writing teachers may find that innovating ways to represent that struggle on the page, whether within the space of the essay or in corollary experimental-poetic practices, helps one accomplish a kind of truthfulness, immediacy, and accuracy in written expression that, paradoxically, will improve the soundness of a thesis, evidence, and conclusion. Just like her recognition that mania manifests a heightened interpretive faculty that can aid in resolving the manic episode, Stecopoulos suggests that poetics can work homeopathically, in line with medical models that see the articulation of an illness not as something to be suppressed but as indication that the body is working to fight something off. The itch, rash, spasm or sneeze that disrupts the illusory stasis of the healthy body is itself an expression and verification of the healthy body. Such visceral adjustments are not disruptions at all. They are part of how the body expresses itself as body, and also as text. The itch, rash, spasm and sneeze are integral to the work of the essay just as they belong to the interpretive work of recovery. To define what is a good argument based upon the achievement of an even procession—without any hiccoughs—from initial premise to final conclusion, is perhaps to ignore those interjections from outside that actually help verify the strength of what is said. Stecopoulos observes how the resonance of bodily processes within a text helps to tune it to material reality: "*Sometimes the stutter is the plot*. Artaud stammered as a child; he was affected by facial tremors. Sometimes the stutter is the phatic tuning that opens the channel to the other" (23). An essay that accommodates the body's non-logical verbal expressions—its reflexes, adjustments and phatic gestures—honors the fullness of how discursive reasoning comes to be.

Let us regard writing as a treatment for the discomfort of needing to work something out, needing to know. Perhaps this need is experienced as grief or excitement: in what way can a text vocalize the heartache or arousal that accompanies the activity of coming-to-know? It is when the omissions demanded by convention sever one's writing from the productive discomfort which originated it, that we end up with an essay that talks about the body without using it, or talks about failed systems without disrupting them, or talks about difference while endlessly producing more of the disabling same.

Sick Reading

When I'm unwell, I can grasp neither letter nor sentence because the edges hurt, so my gut tells me to move, albeit slowly. It tells me that grasping for the figures that lie out of my reach only makes things worse, makes me despondent, useless, unfit. My body floats on, despite the hampering of critical acuity, of interpretive consistency, of memory. My skin, muscles and joints comprehend with extra-sensitivity—to touch, to temperature—and so I can take in more information than usual, which guides where I go next. Standing, undressing, eating, peeing—all of it staggers me, each act manifesting such a particular and palpable result that it becomes its own speaker, articulated. In this state my body finds many places to go, though I anticipate none of them. I'm neither efficient nor blundering. With my tender faculties, I'm always ingesting a new condition, which in turn stages another, and I inhabit each as a fully new person with little recollection of the last.

I wrote the above passage during a week-long bout of insomnia. Sleeplessness, for me, is what happens when something troubling in my unconscious wants out. It often strikes me as a mysterious affliction—an invasion, like a cancer— despite the fact that I've been studying the intricacies of how it works for the whole of my adult life. Over the years, I've come to the conclusion that it's a fitting symptomology for someone like me, a writer, whose self-worth rests upon intellectual alertness: the ever-present fear of losing my superpower causes me to lose my superpower. The dilemma is always heightened when the end goal of my writing is to display mastery of a discipline.

A sleepless night is like being sucked into a vortex, whirled about, and atomized into an abundance of stinging concerns, each so overwhelming that you forget yourself, and the darkness helps to blot out where you are, or the fact that you're anywhere at all. Emerging from it—watching the slow progression of dark to light and realizing that you might as well get out of bed now—is always an interesting feeling. I'll find myself glad it's over—glad I survived—and often too dazed and groggy to be anxious about facing a full day without having been renewed by sleep. The day has restored my sense of place, and the quiet sounds otherworldly. As I go about my morning, I attend to the needs of my body always as a being-who-reads, such that the little zings of discomfort—aching knees, tingling headache—produce their own forms of studying attention and shifting interpretive modes or *moods*. The hypersensitivity I experience during states of exhaustion is like a vivid, technicolor re-rendering of the ways my body normally responds to things in its environment. In a well-rested state, these responses will be dampened and will go unnoticed because my energized attention will have a greater reach and will busy itself elsewhere. Perhaps the states of bodily enervation offer up a productive interpretive mode that I wouldn't know of otherwise. Perhaps the "sick" reader, directed by the will of an unsettled body, is able easily to feel her way to meaning, while the "healthy" reader employs what she already knows, using precedent derived from training as means to a logical, conclusive interpretation. It is a mode of reading that opposes any *rationing* of information that would isolate which lines of thinking promise completion and allow one to digest experience in manageable bites.

And yet there is that brusque little word called *work*—so incessantly used and blurrily defined among us artists and writers—that tunnels through the thickly undifferentiated time of sick reading and rears its head, calling for rationing, parceling, an efficient course. Whenever I find myself looking ahead at a stretch of days or weeks in which

I'll be at my desk trying to complete some scholarly project that has a deadline in the foreseeable future, I experience the procession of time in a very particular way. All of my feelings and states—whether awake or asleep, hungry or full, focused or scattered, strong or self-doubting, agile or hampered, dreamy or calculating—inevitably become a part of the writing experience, whether I want them to or not. Even when I am not reading or writing, I am hyper-aware of what feelings or states make me disinclined to do so, because the project looms as a general standard of measure by which I gauge the quality of my days. Somatic interruptions look like saboteurs, getting in the way of "good work," and in bed at night I'll mull over what went wrong.

Holistic Criticism

> I am sick with exit
> to say what ° we are the world the
> dismemberers those names
> mortify my satisfaction

—Eleni Stecopoulos, *Armies of Compassion*

The word "poetics" in Stecopoulos's title says something about the way the dissertation itself speaks, and the particular sort of reflexive analysis it extends. It is not poetry, but one senses the process behind it as a poetic process above all else. Its fragmentary nature—with short sections stitched together within short chapters that bear titles like "The Pasticcio of Parole," "Kontiki Acrobats" and "Of Teratology"—reveals the project's seams and gives it the feeling of something hewn and molded, assembled and reassembled. If I place it alongside Stecopoulos' poetry, the critical attentions of one and the formal attentions of the other bleed into each other.

In the poem above—excerpted from her 2010 collection—a self dis-integrated by chronic pain finds uncertain resolution in the shape of the word "I." The dimension of self that feels the pain and the one that labors to speak it are such irreconcilably different animals that they can't figure out how to approach each other. And the sounds and forms of words seem to occur to the speaker upon prompting by an internal urgency whose communicative tactics defy reason. In a body with crossed wires and constricted channels, words arrive via unexpected pathways—whatever the psyche can innovate to satisfy a craving for representation. Likewise, in Stecopoulos's critical prose, writing moves between different modes in a dynamic demonstration of the struggle to corral thought and feeling in a legible form. This holistic criticism—active both in her poetry and her essays—tracks the body's resistance to logos-as-accounting, and tracks as well the compromise between body and word, to which the existence of the text testifies. It observes the way that one's physical state continually renews how the word works, in accordance with visceral need.

Genre works as a tool for diagnosis, a measure of ability. It creates its own rules and thus its own deficiencies. It is an equation that says what cadences, vocabulary, topics and sentiments will ring deficient or pathological in a given textual space. Against this, Stecopoulos offers her vision of a holistic criticism. Holistic criticism treats what a text expresses not as indication of that writing's genre or mappable type, but as one phase in a continuous movement between wildly varied conditions. This flow is "the poem of how the sympathies and antipathies of fragments play between artifice and organism" (58). Holistic medicine treats the expression of discomfort or pain as one condition in a chain of intelligent somatic responses. It is not certain states that are healthy, but the acceptance of an undeniably evolving state, one that experiences both pleasure and pain. Likewise, both logical clarity and poetic opacity are instructive states of being within a written work. The health of the work is in the life of these conditions responding one to the other.

Thus, against a literary criticism "predicated on repressing that bodies, not minds, write" (59), holistic criticism "follows whatever radiates from a text" (60). In a self-directed challenge spoken in the contrarian voice of her internal critic, or perhaps of the disciplined theorist nauseated by the task of reading another's sick body, Stecopoulos writes:

> *...why would you insist so much on the way writing pervades your body if writing did not signify for you disembodiment, solitude, distancing from other bodies...if writing criticism did not seem to distend your head as an overseeing parasite, feeding off every contact...*I insist on it because the *feeling* of disembodiment can only be known viscerally; to be aware of, to be conscious of feeling disembodied is already a response to the habitus. Writing embodies disembodiment. (59)

The critical writing tradition has regularly chosen not to see what it already knows: that it is overwhelmed by its resistance to bodily states, and that the pressure they assert can be read behind its words. The critical writer inherits a demand for teleological clarity— a course charted by intention—which the essay must perform. But the complex inter-communication between neurological activity and environmental input that constitutes the thinking process out of which the essay is shaped is necessarily haphazard and multidirectional, even in the healthiest of states. When the writer has a coughing fit, a herniated disc, a broken heart, or performance anxiety, the disjunct between the linear argument and the body it belies will be all the wider. The integrity of the plot or course that holds together the well-argued critical intervention is always therefore volatile, still ringing from the cacophony that produced it. Alternatively, holistic criticism recognizes that organs, muscles, bones and skin speak loudly in both the poem intended to channel the body's wishes and the essay that was composed to subdue its voice. The moment when illness or disablement disrupts the habitual functioning of the body or the easy formulation of a sentence, is a moment when new critical faculties enter the scene. Thus, for Stecopoulous, sickness provides paradoxically a critical "edge":*"Hole, whole, heal...* I feared I would no longer be able to write if I were not divided, if I were "healthy"... there would no longer be any fissure or gap, no disturbance (no parasite) by which to mean, no jagged edge by which to enter. And what is an edge if not the critical, a pick-axe with which to choose?" (43).

In a 1965 essay on Nietzsche, Gilles Deleuze makes a similar observation, noting that Nietzsche, having suffered years of disablement from a series of conditions including migraines, temporary blindness, diphtheria, dysentery and syphilis, "saw in illness a *point of view* on health; and in health a *point of view* on illness" (Deleuze 58). Nietzsche viewed the disruption that his various illnesses caused as an escape hatch from the unreflective complacency of equanimity and good health. Likewise, Stecopoulos models a critical writing that grants the body a place both within the fluctuations of pain and pleasure as realized in poetic word play, and within the negative presence of what the essay denies as it perpetuates our longstanding history of wise men bent over books, with "distended heads" like "overseeing parasites." She sketches a "Theory as Vision" (Stecopoulos 40), one that actively looks beyond the text and at the body, which is theory's resident elephant in the room. The struggle to incorporate the invisible body will give rise to its own set of pains and pleasures. Stecopoulos models how the essay can accommodate all of this.

In advocating for a writing that attends to the body of the writer, Stecopoulos makes a case for incorporating into the book what is spatially outside of it. The cerebral practice of criticism will be more truthful, she thinks, if the products of mind are recognized as products of a larger body, an organic system which ought to show itself within the composition. Moreover, the resources that lie outside of and should be folded into literary critical discourse include not just the body of the writer but neighboring disciplines and genres that speak and make meaning in different ways. Stecopoulos's book and the dissertation from which it arose strive toward this form of maximal inclusivity, drawing content from both daily life and a multitude of texts, and incorporating formal strategies from a range of genres including poetry, autobiography and philosophy. Her approach to critical prose embraces a process that is poetic in nature, expanding language's function beyond the performance of logical clarity, and reaching for playful, speculative, intuitive, surrealistic, or para-logical experiments with syntax and sound. This formal expansiveness is one way to address the problem of feeling *unfit* to write during states of diminished health. In grasping for other forms, Stecopoulos reaches toward alternate representational environments where her thinking might find a better fit. The combined pressure of discipline and enforced fitness is something *Visceral Poetics* consciously struggles against, and it is a topic to which her friend and occasional collaborator Robert Kocik devotes extended critical attention in his own book *Supple Science.* There he elaborates a project of "overcoming fitness," an approach to creative and pedagogical work that seeks to resolve the apparent conflict between holism and genre.

Overcoming Fitness

Kocik's writing is never easily categorizable, as his books encompass poems, essays, architectural plans, lecture transcripts, libretti, songs, drawings and other forms. Bookstores classify it as poetry, though no single form ever dominates his work. For him, the poem always has an immediate purpose, and the purpose should suggest the best form for its own articulation. This does more than simply re-affirm the writing teacher's insistence on "knowing your audience"; it is a realization of poetics as a broad attention to all forms of making. The writer who listens broadly will inevitably happen upon subject matter that calls her to build an altar, seed a garden, plan a meeting or teach a class without ever putting a pen to paper, and any one of these would be an act of poetic composition. Kocik practices poetry as a general meditation on making; not a hard science or a soft science but a "sore" or "supple" one.

This supra-generic poetics recognizes genre-affiliation as a tool of empire and exclusion, party to the disabling structures of society which poetic making is positioned to redress. "Overcoming Fitness," an essay first published in 2001 that appears in *Supple Science*, teases out the many ways in which educational, cultural and economic institutions originate both the categories of identification by which fitness is measured, and the fitness morality that punishes distinctive bodies and artworks as deficient. Fitness is a biased assessment tool that pre-determines which affect, voice, posture, gait, vocation, earning potential, gender, ethnicity, sexuality and language will fail to pass as normal. As the valorization of a "greater adaptedness over others in a common, tightly-knit niche" (Kocik 30), fitness pervades the everyday conditions that support our living. Labor—creative or otherwise—cannot be quantified and paid if it doesn't adapt to the qualifying habits of its proper niche or discipline. It is difficult to imagine a world where every possible category of affect, voice, posture, gait, vocation, earning potential, gender, ethnicity, sexuality and language does not already demand its own version of propriety. We are disciplined by genre because without it our work would become de-standardized and unintelligible. And the engineered spaces we inhabit dictate the shapes of our bodies just like the genres, fields, niches and disciplines dictate the shape of our work. Reproducing the instructions given by our conditions will always reproduce fitness and unfitness, ability and disability.

As writers and academics, we are all aware of this hindrance to our freedom of movement, and we try to circumvent it by including as topics of our scholarship those perspectives that have typically been ignored by our institutional disciplines. The establishment of women's studies, indigenous studies, African American studies, queer studies and disability studies departments attest to crucial efforts at expansion. At the same time, they are unable to circumvent fitness, because what they ultimately accomplish is a persuasive case for the fitness of what has otherwise been judged to be unfit. How do we overcome this?

The Non-Affinitive Bond

In a piece he wrote for a proposed anthology of essays on "poetics of disablement," Kocik brings his project of overcoming fitness into dialogue with the academic discipline of disability studies. In that text, entitled "Without Suffering Succession," he admits: "My commitment to disability is disarmingly simple. I've vowed to help where I can, how I can, if I can, and especially if I *can't* (as the only way of overcoming being unable to do so)" (210). In the same text, Kocik quotes Stecopoulos: "Disability founds aesthetics[2]—for all persons, not just those with disabilities. If we became conscious of that, perhaps we might start to see how all our conditions determine our forms" (qtd. in Kocik 211). Artworks arise from the struggle to represent the unrepresentable, from the disablement induced by the fact that given forms of signification have always been tailored for a world that preceded this one in this moment, and for the people we were before we became what we are now. The painting and the poem trace the strain of saying and doing what

---

2. I find it useful to note that the term "aesthetic" originated as an indicator of embodied experience, as the Greek root *aisthanesthai* means "to feel" or "to sense."

can't be said or done. Kocik's work suggests a solution to the "discrepancy between activism and formal poetry innovation" (211): in allowing language a kind of stuttering play that relaxes the demand for transparency and easy communication, poetic experiments suggest the garbled communication that will always occur amid a diverse coalition of people who are trying to negotiate a shared path toward social change (or who are trying collectively to understand a difficult text that has been assigned for homework). Changing the disabling conditions we are in will require moving through a phase of inscrutability. Innovating new relations to our conditions, mutually helping ourselves to the extremes of what is available to thought and action—through constructing buildings that embrace a multiplicity of bodies, or inaugurating experimental institutions, or structuring unprecedented political systems, or communicating with those who speak a different language—will always be a process of productive mutual misunderstanding. This is his poetics.

Such a vision necessitates a great leap. It would demand a turning toward what is inconceivably distant. One of the fundamental poetic tasks Kocik undertakes is to discover the contiguity of opposites through writing. In a discussion of genetic sequencing, he muses about the inanimate chemicals comprising DNA that have given rise to humanity as such: "The immortal code responsible for life itself is inanimate. I find this fact utterly surprising—worth reflecting on for millennia to come—that we arise from the inanimate, are borne by the inanimate and ultimately return to the inanimate—and that our most profound commonality is with the inanimate" (34). This is what he calls the "non-affinitive" or "heterologous" bond; what makes it possible to identify with what we are not and to do what we can't do, allowing us to reach "extremes of accommodation." The importance of exerting this kind of practice cannot be overstated. Likeness and affinity do not facilitate connectivity; they are rather what threaten it most, because they make it easy for the dominion of fitness to swallow relationships into exclusive and commercially exploitable categories of sameness.

Kocik wonders how a text can accommodate what feels most opposite it, wishing to go further than the boundary pushing that has historically characterized avant-garde practice. Edginess—which I'll define as an aesthetic that embellishes the banal and palatable with small measures of strangeness (think a hamburger with kimchi on top)—is a quality to which businesses and other institutions aspire as they strive to articulate themselves in a competitive market. Advertising habitually borrows from the avant-garde, building branding campaigns out of forms with which readers, viewers or buyers are familiar, yet with a twist, a small dose of defamiliarization, a hint of exotic mystery. Spend a few minutes watching prime time TV commercials and you'll notice visual and sound motifs derived from contemporary art. The next logical aesthetic step away from where we currently are—the "near side of the norm"—will always be captured within the industry's purview. Kocik's writing exists in a wholly other realm, provoking an extreme defamiliarization that launches far beyond edginess. He utilizes styles, tones, words and inflections that draw from spheres of culture that, to his readers, will have none of the exotic mystery that otherwise lends avant-garde art some degree of consumer appeal. His vocabulary is a cornucopia of invented jargon collaged from markedly non-edgy disciplines such as business, social work, medicine and urban planning, and his stylistic mode alternates between taxonomizing, alliterating, punning and chanting. The result is a textual assemblage that differs so wildly from one moment to the next that it would be impossible to isolate some tasty visual or sonic morsel that could serve to represent what this writing is. It is fundamentally resistant to branding.

The *abnormality* of Kocik's art is in line with his imagining (simultaneously architectural and poetic) of a place where norms are unstable, there is no common language, and everyone flounders. This would be a "disequilibrating" space of "radical facilitation" (Kocik 212). In 2008, Kocik cofounded the Commons Choir with the choreographer Daria Faïn. The choir is a performance group comprised of around thirty dancers, singers, actors, musicians and poets working together to conduct "choreoprosodic research," the findings of which would be publicized by way of performance, symposia and teach-ins (dariafain.net). Combining Faïn's expertise in Chinese Energetics with Kocik's investigations in poetic practice, the choir's performance work utilized both movement and voice in a group compositional dialectic between improvisation and resolute forms. In this process, everyone played, using gestural and linguistic vocabularies that didn't count on logical clarity for activating useful exchange. Rather, a rollicking, spastic, glossolalic, echolalic negotiation unfolded: "accumulation of all the vibrations of exchange" "things coming together and coming apart" "polarities popping up." Meaning, as an independent value pre-dating the play of words in action, was dethroned, humanized, collectivized, localized to give its consumers a better sense of where sustenance derives from and how it is cultivated. This is commoning, "a de-centralized, open-ended, slow-paced, often inefficient form of collaborative listening in which people help each other speak" (Kocik 234). In an "entrainment that includes the movement of bodies in space" (230), dance and speech become a combined investigation of—to quote Stecopoulos once again—"how all our conditions determine our forms."

What I've always appreciated most about postmodern dance improvisation is the image it offers of voluntary blundering. It makes the work of *essaying* into a form in itself, and under these conditions failure doesn't preclude grace. I have myself tried out various forms of collective somatic research, having joined the Commons Choir for a brief time, and otherwise participated in Contemplative Dance Practice, Authentic Movement, Underscore and Soma workshops. In movement improvisation I learn about how infinitely particular and variable are the ways with which each body is equipped to register or *say* its meanings. Seeing how a slight variation in the angle of a joint or the contraction of a muscle can pose a question to be answered by another body with its own inestimable range of subtleties, opens a kind of expressivity that requires sensitivity more than eloquence for its effective communication. I am struck most of all by the unique power to accommodate *fear* that dance practice seems to wield. In group improvisation the fear of ineptitude, humiliation or isolation will manifest on our bodies, either in how we give expression to our fear or in how we try to cover it up.

The body can't help but register its response to other entities in its environment, while words on a page have a built-in pretense to detached self-sufficiency. This irrepressible expressivity of the body is something that the architecture of a classroom is structured to hide, compartmentalize, and redirect. While I'm not interested in outlining a prescription for how to build bodily experience into curricula, I'll emphasize the importance of somehow employing critical thinking and critical writing toward an encounter with what is viscerally discomfiting about the present; which, in the classroom, will palpably resonate a long history of institutional demands and exclusions. I see such a reckoning as a crucial learning goal. In academic settings, much of the pressure we assert on other people—to articulate better, to use language in an organized fashion, to defend a position, to change an opinion—is an unconscious redeployment of the punishing tactics that we're so accustomed to using on ourselves. Reflexive investigation will be a first step toward the possibility of producing intellectual work that isn't unconsciously shaped by the pressures and resistances that our institutional inheritance imposes.

What Stecopoulos and Kocik's writing accomplishes for me is a rejection of writing's pretense to unadulterated logos—of its promise to capture ideas in a realm untouched by the vagaries of the body—and an activation of the essay's capacity to show its own vulnerability in the face of the very real world it addresses. It allows writing to grope around where it isn't certified to go, more phatic and haptic than confidently correct.

The Story Illness Tells

When I made the decision to quit the recommended treatments for my sleeplessness, I had to take what I didn't like about how I felt as an irrefutable part of me, no longer separating it out as a defect that could be wiped away by medicines prescribed by experts. Nobody had the means to cure me because my symptoms were inextricable from the countless twists and turns of a thirty-plus year history lived in this body. Practically speaking, it meant I was looking at a future in which I would be contending daily with the discomfort of something that felt like illness instead of trying to artificially dampen the symptoms when they arose.

My purpose in recounting this has to do with how it ultimately bore upon my relationship to reading and writing. At the time, my days presented a continued struggle to reconcile my long-established identity as a writer with the fact that letting my body work out its own problems was leaving me feeling cloudy, exhausted, forgetful and blank; it seemed impossible to welcome my condition and also remain fit for intellectual exertion. But because I no longer believed in the medicine, I had no choice, so I attempted the work, and it was mostly agonizing; a daily extended reminder of my seemingly incurable defects. I thought that if I kept at it I could find a way through, and I resolved to read William James's writings on psychology, hoping that his introspective philosophical style might serve the double purpose of satisfying my intellectual hunger while helping me heal myself. As I dove into the 1400-plus-pages of *The Principles of Psychology* and his later writings in *Essays in Radical Empiricism*, I found myself affected by the following passage, from the essay "Does Consciousness Exist":

> If the reader will take his own experiences, he will see what I mean. Let him begin with a perceptual experience, the "presentation," so called, of a physical object, his actual field of vision, the room he sits in, with the book he is reading as its centre; and let him for the present treat this complex object in the commonsense way as being "really" what it seems to be, namely, a collection of physical things cut out from an environing world of other physical things with which these physical things have actual or potential relations. Now at the same time it is just those self-same things which his mind, as we say, perceives; and the whole philosophy of perception from Democritus's time downwards

has just been one long wrangle over the paradox that *what is evidently one reality should be in two places at once*, both in outer space and in a person's mind. (James 7)

James's resolution of this paradox invokes a concept that is key to his philosophy of pragmatism, which theorizes "pure experience" as the constant interplay between physical encounter and reflective process. Upon reading, I found that the teaching contained in this narrative moment was enacted in real time by the particular way in which I was affected by it. In experiencing a text *look at me* in such a way—as the passage exactly described the literal situation of my body in space as I read it—I began to see the book as a gesture of love, one that didn't brandish its complexity before my intellect like a prize I could possess only by means of an adequately athletic feat of reason, but revealed its conceptual intricacies as the signposts of an unfolding struggle: that of the reader's bodymind encountering its own knots.

In the beginning of *The Principles of Psychology*, James makes a case for introspective philosophy: "the looking into our own minds and reporting what we there discover" (185). (Stecopoulos formulates a version of this practice as "autoethnography in real time.") His writings formalize this work as philosophical practice, while also maintaining that introspection and reflection are instinctual, ongoing activities that define the very nature of what it is to be human. We are always aware of our own thoughts, while awareness is often a sensation more than it is a cogitation. "The Stream of Thought," perhaps the most famous chapter in *Principles*, describes how one thought always senses and crosses over into another, and thinking thus flows in a stream rather than in a succession of discrete thoughts. To try to zero in on a moment of thinking will always require one to attend to surrounding (preceding and ensuing) thoughts—James calls this the "fringe" of thinking—and thus there will be no zeroing in, as one will be led on a search that meanders in every which way. The more lively the thinker feels, the faster the stream will flow. But what happens when we are sick, fatigued or depressed? James writes:

> in states of extreme brain-fag the horizon is narrowed almost to the passing word,—the associative machinery, however, providing for the next word turning up in orderly sequence, until at last the thinker is led to some kind of a conclusion. At certain moments he may find himself doubting whether his thoughts have not come to a full stop; but the vague sense of a *plus ultra* makes him ever struggle on towards a more definite expression of what it may be; whilst the slowness of his utterance shows how difficult, under such conditions, the labor of thinking must be. (247)

When the mind is fresh, it sees more, looking far ahead of the present thought even while still thinking it. The mind races toward the horizon which glows in the clarity of thought's bright vision. On the other hand, the weary mind sees not much more than what concerns it in the present, rimmed with a dim halo. Under these circumstances, though its perspective may be diminished, thinking is never arrested because it will always sense the arrival of the next thing. Maybe in states of "extreme brain-fag" there is a special kind of consciousness that the spry mind will deactivate. Maybe it is here we are able to have the bare recognition of the thing just one step beyond, because here more than anywhere else we can see and feel the shape of it as it is—the *plus ultra*—as if emerging from the blankness of an emptied-out self.

The complexity of James' topics paired with his introspective, illustrative, and often genial style has the effect of affirming that all readers' bodyminds are intricately knotted, and that to move through the concepts with ease would be to understand nothing at all, as it would skirt the hard work of consciousness in action reflecting on itself. This is the overall shape of the critical work that his writings do. Thinking's constant fight to find representation, to be written and read, is painstakingly narrated in an oeuvre whose process of composition was to document the unfolding of that same struggle in the author.

The nonstop work of reading my own body, which became necessary once I realized diagnoses were not facilitating my recovery, *needed the defects* in order to understand and re-balance the whole. Noticing the context of each bout of cloudiness or confusion— what dietary choices, levels of stress or physical activity, and emotional events in my social life may have prompted the state I was in—was my learning path, and I needed to dwell in and move through the cloudiness and confusion in order to approach my goal of informed self-help. The demonstration of that very process is the raison d'être in much of James's work. Any hitch I experienced in trying to comprehend his flow of ideas was itself something that would help my understanding as it exemplified the kind of cognitive tangle that his writing strives to illuminate. The analytical powers I discovered as a "sick reader" enabled a similar kind of readerly and writerly freedom to what Stecopoulos describes in *Visceral Poetics*. Letting the fullness of my condition express itself, I found my discomfort to be "at once a disease and the very sign of my power to find the way out of the labyrinth" (Stecopoulos 11).

On Alien Grounds

I'd like to take a sharp turn here toward the writing of a very different thinker from James. The following passage comes from the queer theorist and disability activist Eli Clare, in his 2017 book *Brilliant Imperfection*:

> Having shaky hands and shaky balance isn't as awful as they imagine, even when I slip, totter, descend stairs one slow step at a time. My relationship to gravity is ambivalent. On mountain trails, I yearn to fly downhill, feet touching ground, pushing off, smooth and fluid. Instead on steep stretches I drop down onto my butt and slide along using both my hands and feet, for a moment becoming a four-legged animal. Only then do I see the swirl marks that glaciers left in the granite, tiny orange newts climbing among the tree roots, otherworldly fungi growing on rotten logs. My shaky balance gives me this intimacy with the mountain. (87-89)

Clare reveals the complicated personal and political questions one faces when seeking to medically cure a bodily condition. As an activist, he wants better healthcare for people with disabilities; at the same time he realizes that the cultural obsession with medically "fixing" the body is detrimental to his vision of a truly pluralistic world, one that spans a range of bodily shapes and appearances without elevating one type as the best. The above passage represents both a longing for capacities he doesn't have and a love for the avenues of experience opened by the particular way in which his body works. Like Stecopoulos' "autoethnography in real time" and Kocik's "choreoprosodic research," Clare's mode of thinking and composing in *Brilliant Imperfections*—which includes periodic forays into lineated poetry, with a poem appearing at the beginning of each chapter—is an effort of intense and ceaseless study of oneself in the world, in which the daily difficulties of being a body become fascinating and instructive even while they are painful. They bring him in contact with other languages, the sign systems of rocks and tree roots with the ancient stories they tell, and show him that each perceived limit to how he moves, thinks, feels or creates is instead a new terrain to inhabit. One can approach the threshold and feel around there, touching and testing the lay of the land at the edges of what is tolerable. An investigative dwelling in the realm of what one *can't do* as a way to annul the imperative of fitness and debunk the hegemonic ideologies of which it is an expression.

Pressure to *overcome* one's body is ubiquitous in the narratives perpetuated by the medical industrial complex, to use Clare's term. I quote him again here:

> Overcoming bombards disabled people. It's everywhere. I think of Whoopi Goldberg. In airports and along freeways, I see her plastered on a billboard sponsored by the Foundation for a Better Life (FBL). Head in hands, dreadlocks threaded through fingers, she furrows her forehead in frustration. Or is it bemusement? She casts her eyes up, looking directly at her viewers. The tagline reads, "Overcaem dyslexia," coyly misspelling *overcame*. Underneath those two words brimming with stereotypes sits a red box containing the phrase "HARD WORK," and below that, the command "Pass It On." (8)

The message is clear: Goldberg traversed the difficult path to stardom and success despite her defect, and her renown evidences a remarkable triumph over a cognitive quirk that should have kept her among the ranks of other needy, defective, unknowns. On the contrary, Clare wonders if it was the othered idiosyncrasies of her body and mind that enabled a wide range of "abnormal" perceptive strengths that shaped her comedic talent.

The medical industrial complex renders as mighty heroes those who endure the therapies and medicines—which are often disabling themselves—that promise a path to normalization. It depicts the innate, brilliant imperfections of all bodies—our instructive coughs and hiccoughs, and even our deaths—as defects to be conquered. On the contrary, Clare presses the point that what appears as an intellectual or physical shortcoming is often the very quality that energizes and refines one's processes of thought or action. This was indeed the case in my experience of reading James and reading the daily ups and downs of my own body amid the ongoing work of recovery.

That work, without the intervention of external therapeutic mechanisms promising a "fix" —pharmaceutical or otherwise—led to the discovery that *my alleged defects were necessary for good reading comprehension.* Whenever my understanding butted up against a phrase in James that felt particularly dense or opaque, I experienced this as a bit of physical pain, an acidic burn in my skull and a bracing compaction of the vertebrae. It was my habitual policing of my own cognitive fitness that provoked these panic symptoms, and in recognizing the effort I exerted to discipline my own seeming limitations, I realized that the defect was actually generated by my propensity to self-punishment.

So I sat with what was troubling to me about my somatic state as it contended with the abstraction of words on a page, and it was then that the words resolved into meaning.

The medical preoccupation with fixing the body mirrors the pedagogical tradition of treating the classroom as a place for molding minds. Scholars Rhiannon Firth and Andrew Robinson turn to the work of proto-anarchist Max Stirner in order to elaborate why implementing programs for molding the development of students—however progressive the program might be—might actually hinder the path to self-actualization. To Stirner, a person becomes self-actualized after two major developmental shifts: first, the compulsory sacrifice of one's inborn, singular, experiential intelligence to the forms of thought encouraged by dominant social constructions; second, the shedding of those imposed forms when one is finally able to uncover the buried corporeal self (Firth and Robinson 60-61). Firth and Robinson argue that when teachers are fixated on molding their students to exhibit particular behaviors and thought patterns, the second key developmental shift will be inhibited; for it is only after a student gains practice in allowing her embodied intelligence to discover on its own which behaviors and thought patterns will be efficacious for her unique trajectory in life that she may genuinely become a self (63).

At the crux of my investigation is a belief that the finality implied by the term critical writing—with its assumption that the activity of critique can be captured on a page, frozen in time, its various moments nested hypotactically to create a neat logical map—is at odds with the shapeshifting condition of being a body in the world, a body whose chemistry, dimensions, mood and climate are continuously overhauled by the influence of its environment. Any act of writing is to some degree a straightjacketing of cognition and all its concomitant visceral processes. This subjects the body's consciousness to an experience of alienation, which can feel rather uncomfortable. But one feels it in the body, and that pain brings the mind back home. To quote Stecopoulos once again: *writing embodies disembodiment* (59). The pain of feeling straightjacketed is perhaps a claustrophobic death-anxiety, where the incomprehensible inevitability of the body's cessation can only be imagined as a kind of cramping enclosure. *Visceral Poetics* sees this truncation of somatic experience as a necessary and instructive component of what the bodymind knows.

Critical writing cannot help but truncate critical thinking, and thus the essay I assign my students to write is wrong before it is written. Since no writing can perfectly "demonstrate" the multi-directional breadth of critical thinking, perhaps the purpose of the essay is not to demonstrate thinking at all but to carve out a space in which the author can consciously encounter the various existential contradictions embedded in the lie which says the self is composed of a mind governing the actions of a body. The essay has the capacity to reveal to the writer her own alienation, to make her feel it in her body. Stecopoulos, Kocik and Clare all recognize that the widespread belief in a detached mind that governs the body functions as a tool for colonizing somatic intelligence. And underlying the teacher's wish to instill in a student the ability to correctly represent her thoughts on paper is the conviction that one ought to overcome the discomfort of feeling alienated within the language one is given.

But perhaps alienation is itself educational. Perhaps the ill-adapted are the ones best equipped to see their conditions acutely for what they are. Our social institutions have historically pathologized the resistance effected by those who can't or won't be molded into shape. Clare cites examples of this, beginning with the writings of 19th century physician Samuel Cartwright, who diagnosed the "problem" of enslaved Africans trying to escape bondage as a "disorder" called *drapetomania*, and their persistent unwillingness to work, even under the whip, as *dysaesthesia aethiopica* (24). The 60s era psychiatrists Walter Bromberg and Frank Simon saw "specific reactive psychoses" in the members of Civil Rights and Black Power movements, referring to the phenomenon using the general term "protest psychosis" (Clare 24). This tradition of viewing defiance as a medical disorder is perpetuated in the practice of pathologizing and punishing the "inability" of students to perform in the context of the institutions where they are educated. Some so-called defects need to be recognized as marks of conscious or unconscious resistance. If the resistance appears to lack intentionality or specific aim, it is because power works hard to make itself invisible and one often doesn't see the constellation of forces that combine to cause a feeling of powerlessness. Perhaps the source is too complex to be seen at all. But one must try. It is important for the critical writer to have the time and space to dwell attentively within his or her "defects."

All acts of scholarship and writing manifest failed messages, trite formulations, ill-defended points, missed points, misplaced or displaced dialects and maladroit grammars that may contain a great deal of information about what authority the writer struggles against. What if the student writer and the writing teacher were to momentarily pause their institutionally-imposed, harsh self-assessments so as to value their alleged failures as information, and, with a rigorous scholarly eye, attend to them as necessary details within a larger emerging picture?

The notion of a well-argued essay is utopian, and such an ideal requires the consent to a certain fantasy: that of some reality, firmly and sustainably built upon reason, in which the fundamental unreason of the body bears no influence, or belongs to a different plane altogether. Learning to construct such an edifice is a useful intellectual exercise, but it will always be hypothetical, and require a temporary insensitivity—a kind of writerly sociopathy. This is because the writer is also a nervous system affected by temperature, quality of light, ambient sound, and perhaps most importantly, the interjection of other bodies with their own visceral realities. The essay is a pact with the reader in which both parties agree, for a duration, to imagine dwelling in a world that is devoid of those variables. The argument produced in black lettering and framed by the crisp edges of a white page, wants to temporarily displace and defer all of that input—wants to be airtight. Writers like Stecopoulos, Kocik, Clare and, to some degree, James, attend to these excisions through poetry, or through a hybrid poetic-essayistic practice. Experimental processes can help give airtime to somatic digressions, resistances, and contingencies. Writing can be implemented to honor the asides—the thoughts one has while trying to concentrate on the topic, the bodily pains that announce themselves during the struggle to think clearly, the daydreams that pop up, the series of wrong words and discarded phrases that precede the final form, the nonsense that the mind kicks up during the work of producing sense. These are not byproducts: they're the very fabric of thought. One can use experiments on the page to dwell within them.

When thinking stops at some logical leap that is needed in order to arrive at an intended point and the pressure to exhibit an impeccably polished intellect manifests as a headache, a hot flash, or some other somatic expression, try relocating micro-essays in the margins of your writing that excavate how a particular thought has registered in the body. Borrow automatic writing prompts from the surrealists. Take cues from the concrete poets and treat the composition of thought spatially, activating the white space of the page. Write a list poem, representing thoughts as a sequence of complex nouns, each one a new creature giving birth to the next. Turn on a recording device and narrate the sensation of thinking as it unfolds. Listen to the recording and write in response to the sounds of the words you hear, the cadence and texture of your voice. Verbally address another body so as to remind yourself that thinking doesn't happen in a vacuum, and that the gnawing critical conundrum isn't simply your own. Write with your eyes closed. Take a walk; consider how the momentum of thinking changes in accordance with the motion of the body through space. I don't guarantee that any of this will produce writing that is beautiful, but in exploring compositional practices that transcend ideologies of success and failure, ability and disability, we reckon with the systems of subordination that operate inside and over us; to me, this seems to be the most urgent thing.

Works Cited

Clare, Eli. *Brilliant Imperfection: Grappling with Cure.* Duke University Press, 2017.

Deleuze, Gilles. *Pure Immanence: Essays on A Life.* Translated by Anne Boyman, Zone Books, 2005.

"The Commons Choir." *Daria Fain*, http://www.dariafain.net/commons-choir. Accessed 19 July 2024.

Firth, Rhiannon and Andrew Robinson. "From the Unlearned Un-man to a Pedagogy without Moulding: Stirner, Consciousness-Raising, and the Production of Difference." *Out of the Ruins: The Emergence of Radical Informal Learning Spaces,* edited by Robert H. Haworth and John M. Elmore, PM Press, 2017, pp. 56-73.

James, William. "Does Consciousness Exist." *Essays in Radical Empiricism*, edited by Ralph Baron Perry, University of Nebraska Press, 1996, pp. 1-38.

—. *The Principles of Psychology.* Harvard University Press, 1983.

—. "World of Pure Experience." *Essays in Radical Empiricism*, edited by Ralph Baron Perry, University of Nebraska Press, 1996, pp. 39-91.

Kocik, Robert. *Supple Science: A Robert Kocik Primer.* Contemporary Practice, 2013.

Stecopoulos, Eleni. *Visceral Poetics.* Contemporary Practice, 2016.

JAEPL, Vol. 29, 2024

Echo and Drag as Resistance: Coloniality, Queerness, and Practices of Reading Student Texts

Joshua Barsczewski and Florianne Jimenez

Abstract: *In this article, a postcolonial theorist and a queer studies scholar reconsider the role of student resistance in Writing Studies' social justice turn, arguing for a way of reading student texts that accounts for why students might choose to take up social justice or not in their own writing. Through examples from their ongoing research projects, the writers discuss how students' resistance surfaced not as visible and explicit signs of a changed epistemological framework or political perspective, but as a series of normative rhetorical choices that made space for more transgressive or subversive possibilities.*

In recent years, writing studies has been undergoing what Pritha Prasad and Louis M. Maraj describe as a "social justice turn" that centers marginalized writers, specifically their texts, theories, and rhetorical strategies as they experience and, in some cases, redress inequity and oppression (326). Similarly, a recent collection entitled *Writing Democracy: The Political Turn in and beyond the Trump Era* calls for an explicitly "political" turn, where teachers and scholars use Marxist theory and draw "insight and strength from historical struggles for social and economic justice in labor, civil rights, Black Power, women's rights, and national liberation struggles" (Carter, Mutnick, Parks, and Pauszek 2). While the Trump presidency is one nexus around which the political or social justice turn has certainly become exigent, the desire for politically engaged teaching and scholarship that draws strength from activist movements can be found throughout the larger history of writing studies, including its long engagement with critical pedagogy and the broadly recognized "social turn" (Boyd; Bizzell). Indeed, the trajectory from a "social" paradigm to "social justice" or "political" one can be seen as less of a distinct turn and more so a series of overlapping, sometimes fuzzy, and often conflated circles of conversation that have been developing since at least the 1970s Open Admissions movement. As new social and political problems became obvious, the discipline's approach to teaching and research shifted: from a focus on access to higher education, to teaching about social justice topics, then to developing systems of engagement between academic and nonacademic spaces, to more recently reconsidering how different forms, styles, and genres of writing can intervene in political affairs (Kinney, Girshin, and Bowlin; Rhodes and Alexander).

This article is not interested in critiquing the goal of these "turns" or pedagogical initiatives. Indeed, both authors agree that students need and deserve teachers attuned to social justice, given the realities of an increasingly militant right wing, a noted rise in anti-Black and anti-Asian violence, publicly visible displays of Nazi idolatry, nationwide movements for anti-immigrant and anti-trans legislation, and education policies in places like Florida that enact explicitly racist, homophobic, and transphobic curricula. What we do want to interrogate, however, is how social justice takes rhetorical form in students' texts. Specifically, we worry about what we see as a rather pressing conflation in the social justice turn: the extent to which agency has become equated with explicit and visible signs of students' resistance to oppressive power structures in their writing.

In *Writing Democracy*, for instance, contributors describe how business writing classes can be involved in community outreach (Clegg) and argue that teachers should "work with labor, social justice activists, and local publics to develop and/or join existing projects for freedom and democracy" (Mutnick 91). These examples engage students in what Ingo Winkler and Irma Rybnikova call "critical-emancipatory" resistance, or resistance that imagines and works toward changes in power relations beyond just the classroom walls (528). Other types of critical-emancipatory resistance in the classroom would include: writing critically about social issues in a way that reflects progressive viewpoints, pushing back against linguistic normativity and conventional academic discourse, engaging in critique of power structures, and emulating social and political activism from the public sphere. Students who can engage with writing in this way visibly demonstrate what teachers might hope are altered epistemological frameworks that can be harnessed as part of a move toward increased civic participation and activism more broadly (Liu and Tanacito; Harrington and Wheeler).

There is, then, an economy of visibility and legibility at play in social justice writing pedagogy. Critical-emancipatory resistance exists if we can see signs of it and when we can see students applying knowledge about the world's injustices to write about or intervene in them. However, can all students answer the call for resistance equally? What about marginalized students who have good reasons to distrust the pedagogical apparatuses of the classroom, and who thus decide that the classroom is not a worthwhile space to demonstrate their political beliefs, as doing so poses safety issues? Or perhaps they have reason to distrust that anything meaningful will result from critical inquiry or expression given the institutionalized context of the classroom. When and how should teachers know if their social justice pedagogy is working?

In this article, we argue that critical-emancipatory resistance begins with an analysis of power, including the layers of power inherent to students' rhetorical context. Thus, rather than visibly and clearly answering their teacher's call for/to social injustice, students might use their critical skills to instead adopt other rhetorical strategies meant to occlude their teachers. Our contention is that some students are already engaging in this work, with or without our guidance, and that any teacher invested in social justice pedagogy needs to imagine that they might be part of the oppression a student wishes to resist.

To make this argument, we will describe examples from our research projects where we saw students enacting resistance through deployment of conventionality and normativity that could seem acquiescent, but which is instead imbued with a critical analysis of academic context, one allowing them to push back against power relations both in and beyond their immediate rhetorical situation. Florianne's ongoing research project, *Echoing + Resistant Imagining: Filipino Student Writing Under American Colonial Rule*, focuses on the colonized Philippines (1898-1946) and explores how oppressive conditions—legal, social, political, and discursive—shaped the discourse students produced in the writing classroom. The project uses postcolonial theory to analyze the power relations between colonizer and colonized as they manifest in the material conditions and, more crucially, the material risks involved in expressing resistant views as marginalized subjects. She asks, *Under oppressive conditions, and in the colonizer's tongue, how do the colonized write?* Joshua's ongoing research considers the emphasis on anti-normativity in queer composition theory by focusing on the material complexities of LGBTQ+ students' lives. Anti-normativity, in the form of resistance to political conservatism, cisheteronormativity, and even the logics of academic writing itself, is a mainstay of Queer Composition (Banks; Waite; Alexander and Rhodes; Palmeri). Yet, he worries that this emphasis avoids engaging with the material complexities of LGBTQ students' lives, especially trans students who have solid reason to doubt their safety and students of color whose experiences of gender and sexual norms might not fit into white, cisgender narratives of the anti-normative. In both of our research projects, we see multiple examples of students resisting oppression, but not necessarily in ways their teachers would recognize. In fact, in many cases, avoiding detection by their teacher is a *goal*. The social justice turn, thus, should develop ways of reading student texts that enable us to recognize the political potentiality of student writing in new ways and better account for the factor of individual agency in assessments of criticality.

"Resistance" and Students in the Writing Classroom

Although "resistance" to oppression has become understood as a student need under the social justice turn, the larger scholarly trajectory about resistant students has been less certain, especially in scholarship around critical pedagogy. At times, resistant students were understood as obstacles to a teachers' attempts to foster critical thinking. In other words, students pushed back against their teachers' social-justice pedagogies and thus became subjects in need of management/correction. Gwen Gorzelsky, for example, points to a need for teachers to foster students' "ownership of their developing ideas and texts" to avoid students' outright resistance, which is understood as disengagement with or rejection of critical pedagogy (66). The possibility of students resisting and thus rejecting critical pedagogy has also been discussed by Richard Miller, for example, who pointed out that despite his attempts at using Freirean pedagogy, many of his students "resisted the 'politicization' of the classroom" and that "those who didn't seemed overly eager to ventriloquize sentiments they didn't believe or understand" (11). Other scholars have discussed the danger of students resisting their teachers' identities, embodiment, and politics: Karen Kopelson's advocacy of performing neutrality in the classroom came out of a critique of critical pedagogy for its "inattention to differences among classroom rhetorical contexts and among teacher subject positions within those contexts" which made it unable to "meet the challenges posed by today's specific formations of student resistance" (117)[1]. These depictions suggest that students' resistance to a teacher's attempts to educate them are a resistance to the larger good a teacher can do for them.

---

1. Kopelson, interestingly, returned to the idea of performing objectivity in 2020 as a means of "rehabilitating reality" in the Trump years. Unlike her 2003 article, where she worried that students expected academic neutrality and would resist anything that veered from it, she now points out that students expect academics to perform progressivism. The performance of objectivity or neutrality is still, then, a way to forestall student resistance, albeit for different reasons.

However, this is not the only valence such seemingly conforming texts may register. In her influential essay, Mary Louise Pratt has proposed a category of "literate arts of the contact zone" (37)—writing that pushes back against the dominant order through "unsolicited oppositional discourse, parody, resistance, critique" (39). In particular, Pratt's notion of the "autoethnographic text," where writers engage in "selective collaboration with and appropriation of idioms of the metropolis or the conqueror" (35), also restores agency to students by viewing textual acquiescence or compliance with the dominant structure as a possibility for resistance. We also imagine, following Mary Reda, the possibility of "genuine, positive student resistance" as that which can be justified as a "kind of political action" to change their own possibly unbearable or unreasonable pedagogical environments (46). Reda's act of critical imagining forces us to contend with the possibility that our own classrooms are a space where students' resistance is potentially justified and potentially even productive. Reda's insights are also echoed in Cheryl Glenn's work on silence, which has long argued against the prioritization of spoken (and thus apparent or explicit) language as an indicator of resistance, pointing out that silence can be a "strategic choice" and not just an "enforced position" (13). More recently, J. Logan Smilges's work on "queer silence," which they define as "the surprising potentialities of silence to generate meaning from absence and the ways people on the margins of society tap into these potentialities in order to build community, navigate hostile spaces, and resist forms of institutional and state-sponsored violence," opens up conceptual pathways for understanding silence not just as an intentional rhetorical choice that one can employ, but as a way of being, existing, and making meaning. In doing so, Smilges highlights the problematic economy of legibility undergirding rhetorical theory's prioritization of speaking and instead calls for scholars to shift "away from what people are saying to what they aren't, away from who is speaking to who is remaining silent, and away from speech entirely toward the way silence has been signifying all along" (9).

In the vein of Glenn, Smilges, and Reda, alongside Winkler and Rybnikova, we imagine possibilities for critical-emancipatory resistance that may not rest on an economy of legibility and visibility; instead, we embrace a view of student resistance that makes space for how students' words may echo the very discourses that oppress them, or a view of student resistance that makes space for how students' engagement of normative discourses may not be an act of compliance, but one of drag. Both theoretical concepts, echo and drag, coming to us from postcolonial and queer perspectives, respectively, nonetheless share the foundational understanding that texts are not transparent indicators but strategic techne at work within a broad framework of student literate activity and agentive positioning.

Florianne: Echoing + Resistant Imagining

My ongoing project examines archival documents written by students at an American-style public school in the Philippines during the early 1900s. After defeating Spain in the Spanish American War, the United States took possession of Spain's colonies: Puerto Rico, Guam, Cuba, and the Philippines. In the Philippines, the U.S. positioned itself as a "benevolent" and "liberating" colonizer[2] compared to Spain, which had ruled the Philippines for 400 years through feudalism and Catholic doctrine. As part of American benevolence via enlightenment, U.S. politicians built an American-style public school system, run entirely by U.S. administrators and teachers. The schools were explicitly designed to indoctrinate students into American language, ways of being, and cultural norms.

In the archives, I saw multiple moments where Filipino students' writings reflected the voices and perspectives of American colonialism. For example, one student, Victor Obleñas, wrote an essay entitled "Civilization of the Philippines" that adheres to the discourses of the oppressor. The essay narrates the Philippines' transition from Spanish colonial rule to American colonial rule, with both colonizers described in glowing terms. To describe Spanish colonization, Victor writes: "My tongue can hardly utter a word when I think of our obligation to Spanish Civilization, for they lightened our dark minds and showed us how to face the real world which God created…" (53). In this description, the student creates a subservient relationship between Filipinos and Spain: the arrival of the Spanish colonizers provided wisdom and truth to ignorant Filipinos. According to Victor, prior to Spanish colonization, the Filipinos were "a warlike people and the powerful chiefs or dattus [sic] conquered the weaker ones" (53). Filipino civilization was a state of brutal disorganization, with the transition of power negotiated by force rather than rationality. Because of other progressive aspects of Spanish colonization such as agriculture and the establishment of schools, Spain was "the first that laid the foundation of our knowledge; the first who opened our minds from ignorance and inspired us with hopes of civilization" (54). When the United States enters the picture, the colonizer/colonized relationship is described in even more effusively positive terms. Victor writes, "My heart is now filled with gratitude, for the United States is constantly holding us in the path of usefulness while she teaches us anxiously with her heart full of love" (57). Victor repeats the relationship of obligation to colonial rule that he expresses towards Spain: he positions the United States as a wholly benevolent nation that "loves" the Philippines.

When I first saw moments like this during my analysis, I was so thoroughly disturbed by how closely they echoed American aims that I almost abandoned the project altogether. These expressions of support and love for two colonial powers were baffling. I felt troubled by the idea that this project's conclusion could be in direct contradiction to my own political and ethical stances. As a Filipino scholar committed to decoloniality, I felt the need for a lens that would open rather than foreclose the range of readings available for these students' texts.

Homi Bhabha's theory of mimicry is one such lens. Mimicry, a theory of discursive production under colonial rule, accounts for the power dynamic between colonizer and colonized. Babha defines mimicry as: "the sign of a double articulation; a complex strategy of reform, regulation, and discipline, which 'appropriates' the Other as it visualizes

---

2. Despite this messaging, the United States did commit mass atrocities in the Philippines. See Paul Kramer's *The Blood of Government: Race, Empire, the United States and the Philippines*, Nerissa Balce's *Body Parts of Empire* and Dylan Rodriguez' *Suspended Apocalypse: White Supremacy, Genocide, and the Filipino Condition*.

power" (126). Colonial difference—the distinction between colonized and colonizer upon which imperial power rests—can never be fully effaced. In Bhabha's terms, "mimicry emerges as the representation of a difference that is itself a process of disavowal" (126). I find Bhabha's mimicry illuminating for considering how asymmetrical contexts of power encourage writing that operates within normativity and assimilation, but at the same time is not — and cannot be — swallowed up by the normative order. While Deepika Bahri has discussed how mimicry may have theoretical utility in Writing Studies "for those studying the rhetoric of public discourse, the politics of basic writing classrooms, the production of educated or institutionalized subjectivity, or the production of discourse in any of several situations where power conjoins with the production of knowledge but remains ambiguated by its own contradictions" (72), I would also caution against too quickly using Bhabha's ideas across all scenes of classroom writing. Bhabha's concept refers to a particular sociohistorical configuration: the taking over of one country and its people by an empire through military, political, and ideological force, primarily for resource extraction. But postcolonial studies recognizes that the effects of colonization are long-lasting: as Victor Villanueva puts it, "There is nothing *post* about the postcolonial in America" (186). As such, Bhabha's notion of mimicry can be taken up by writing studies to consider writing contexts where colonization is a pedagogical drive. Informed by Bhabha's mimicry, I formulated "echoing + resistant imagining" as a writing and rhetorical studies-informed perspective on how the same notes of colonial discourse can appear in writing and discourse across time, media, and space. Unlike mimicry, "echoing + resistant imagining" allows us to *trace* lines of power and influence between and among individuals and institutions.

Being familiar with the depth of colonial damage and trauma, as well as the vibrant history of resistance on the part of Filipinos, "echoing + resistant imagining" allows me to read Victor and other students' texts with more complexity beyond concluding that they believed in empire. Rather, this stance was only one among multiple possibilities available to students at that particular historical moment. Deeper immersion into the material and discursive conditions that surrounded the schools reminded me that this echoing was almost inevitable. These schools were operating at a time of local and global geopolitical tension: as such, Filipino native opposition to American rule was held with suspicion. Laws were eventually enacted that punished Filipino resistance in any form. In November 1901, for instance, the Philippine Commission—an administrative body comprising American bureaucrats who ran the colonies—enacted the Sedition Law, which included advocacy for Filipino independence as an act against the state (Kramer 138). These oppressive conditions surrounded the colonial schools and, I imagine, shaped what students could and couldn't say and write in the classroom without risking material consequences. Displaying open defiance could mean facing disciplinary action at school, marginalization, or, at very worst, legal repercussions.

Global and national geopolitical contextualization matter because a recognition of the conditions under which students write—what they have to gain and lose from writing—allows us to see, as scholars and teachers, negotiating power as an inherent facet of students' writing lives. In other writing that argues for "echoing + resistant imagining," I demonstrated that in colonial situations, there can be a rhetorical function in replicating or mirroring discourses that seem oppressive: "even while it may sound like colonized writers are replicating discourses that support colonial domination, or championing frameworks that position the colonized as savage, backward, or antiquated, [a reading framework of] echoing + resistant imagining calls attention to what else the colonized may be saying beyond questions of acquiescence or subversion" (44-45). For example, when we read an instance of student writing as synecdoche of a student's actual ideological position, we as teachers can miss less obvious strategies of resistance the text is performing. Capitulation to oppressive discourse is certainly a possibility, but I argue that reading for what the *function* of writing could be, rather than reading for what such writing is saying about student political identity, yields a more generous and open stance towards such writing. To return to the case of Victor's essay, for example: we can concede that his view of the colonization of the Philippines by Spain and the US is in overwhelmingly positive terms. However, closer examination of the frame with which he describes US colonialism demonstrates an epistemology of the colonial project as a process suffused with feeling and affect. To be colonized is to be made to feel a certain way, to colonize a country is to be motivated by certain other feelings. This epistemology pushes up against the framing of US colonization as reasoned, logical, and intellectually progressive—and a subtle interruption to other American notions and discourses surrounding the US's relationship to the Philippines at the time.

The theory of echoing + resistant imagining thus asks more of us as we read: we must reckon with how capitulation can be a rhetorically savvy and materially rewarding choice for students. Moreover, to include capitulation to and support for coloniality as an agentive move on students' part recognizes the totalizing nature of coloniality: there is no world where students were or are not aware of the political tensions surrounding coloniality at school, as well as the real stakes involved in success or failure of navigating these tensions.

Joshua: Academic Drag and LGBTQ+ Resistance

My research focuses on the experience of students writing specifically about their identities in classroom settings. Commited to queer pedagogy and social justice teaching, I have been inspired by moments when students in their writing connect their own experiences of gender and sexuality to analysis of broader structures of power that frame those experiences. My hope was to come up with a set of frameworks through which socially-just teachers could encourage students to explore through writing their experiences and identities, and I wanted to follow students' lead on this development. I interviewed 18 self-identified LGBTQ+ students, then did case studies of select students who supplied me with writing samples from their classes. I chose for case studies those students who claimed in the interview that they wanted to or saw the importance of using academic writing to explore their identities.

However, very little of the work students submitted to me seemed to do so. Only a handful of samples, across hundreds of documents, included explicit references to students' personal experiences at all, let alone their experiences of gender and sexuality. Rather, I saw essay after essay where students used dispassionate, seemingly disinterested and neutral voices.

Some students' samples even used voices or perspectives in opposition to the writer's own identity or political perspective, such as Jude, a trans student who wrote fawningly about Antonin Scalia's legal philosophy in their legal studies class, despite being a leftwing activist off-campus, a rhetorical gesture they attribute to simply being bored with the course curriculum.[3] In an interview, I asked how they felt about opportunities teachers provided to explore personal identity in writing, as opposed to more straightforward, impersonal arguments that are often associated with academic writing; Jude responded by describing their sense of both the promise and putative pointlessness of doing so:

> I came to school and I guess I realized that there were at least some professors who were very supportive and even encouraging of my subverting of the rules. And that was very freeing in a lot of ways. And then once I could really wrap my head around that and start putting it in practice, I realize the limits of doing that. First, it's like, yeah, I can subvert the rules of writing; it's so great. So much freedom. But then I guess once I kind of got over that initial excitement, I was like, but academia still sucks…and people are still dying. It's not enough. Nothing I can do in this school can be enough.

Not all of my participants shared in Jude's nihilistic perspective, but a number of others questioned what the role of academic writing—or any writing done on a college campus—means for larger political goals. One of these participants, Garrett, is someone who committed large chunks of his undergraduate years to activism and queer performance, notably subversive drag performances as part of an artistic collective he founded. Yet, in his numerous courses on gender and sexuality, he occasionally lapsed into normative frameworks of analysis, such as an essay for his queer performance class on the concept of "mopping" in ballroom and drag queen culture. Mopping, a practice of stealing garments and dresses—often from department stores or designers—to wear to balls and pageants was a way for economically disadvantaged performers to keep up the illusion of wealth and glamor so idolized in ballroom and drag culture. Garrett's initial essay, which disapproved of the practice for its illegality (he described it as "essentially shoplifting") struck me, for the legalistic framework that declares such a practice deviant seemed at odds with other, more critical lenses he might have taken. In our interview several years after he wrote it, I asked him to reflect on how he defined mopping in legalistic terms, and he indicated that his earlier writing came from not having the intellectual resources to analyze the cultural practice from a more systemic perspective. He said:

> Now when I say, "Well, it is 'essentially shoplifting,'" I don't think so. I would now say, "Shoplifting is framed as such by a certain society." Right? I don't think that I would necessarily say this is 'essentially shoplifting' because I think the stakes are higher. When you think about how wealth and capital works, I don't think I had that knowledge then.

---

3. In fact, Jude initially described their writing as an attempt to be contrarian, but in a later interview changed their description of this assignment as a result of trying to keep themselves interested while being "checked out" and "just doing the work to do the work." I describe Jude in greater depth in my article "A Queer Rhetorics Framework for Discourse-Based Interviews," *Composition Forum*, vol. 49, 2022.

After this reflection, he got even more candid and said, "Honestly, I do remember writing this and I was close to the deadline and trying to fill space." It's this latter comment that I find especially fascinating: while it's true that he had likely grown more nuanced in his views between writing the essay and our interview years later, able to analyze mopping as a subversive survival mechanism by economically disadvantaged and marginalized people against wealthy stores and designers, he draws our attention to how in the first place he was writing to complete an assignment for a teacher and needed to fill space with words; whether he agreed with them or not was beside the point.

In that vein, what he said in the first place shouldn't really be understood as indicative of how he thought even at the time. This suggests a type of academic drag, a concept initially coined by Charles E. Morris III (34) but later expanded on by Alyssa A. Samek and Theresa A. Donofrio to describe a containment of "the radical politics associated with queer rhetorical projects" under the guise of professionalism (32-33). In Garrett's case, academic drag is a performance of discursive normativity that gives the illusion of academic coherence and, almost like an intellectual costume, might be different from and perhaps even contrary to how he thinks.

Using the concept of academic drag to understand Garrett and Jude's writing allows us to see spaces in their academic career when students use normative or even conservative language for potentially resistant purposes. For Jude, academic drag highlights the inefficiency of academic writing for effecting real-world change. Whether Jude is right about this is, ultimately, another conversation, and we might entertain the possibility that Jude lapses into a compliance with their own marginalization by producing writing that supports conservative legal philosophy. Instead of compliance, however, Garrett uses his forms of academic drag to save his energy for other types of discourse for which he sees opportunity for political resistance: his artistic performances. By the time he started participating in my study, he had built a reputation for himself on campus as a queer artist and activist, staging in the Fine Arts Building a subversive and explicitly political drag show that commented on environmentalism, toxic masculinity, and gender fluidity. In one memorable sequence, bloody dildos representing Brett Kavanaugh and R. Kelly's severed penises were carried on a silver platter; in another sequence, a dancer was stabbed to death with a spoke from a Shell Oil logo.

To get the funding for this project, Garret wrote a narrowly conceived, highly formulaic grant application to the university's Honors College, situating the performance as a research project on audience behavior. He downplayed how provocative the performance would be (not saying that he planned to use grant money to purchase dildos, for example) but instead described the philosophical and theoretical importance of drag to contemporary theater practitioners, using concepts from Judith Butler, Michel Foucault, Stephen Farrier, and others. He promised to poll his audience on their experiences as "data" he could then analyze:

> …one of my research questions explores what experiences and emotions arise for creators and audience members of ensemble-based narrative drag and queer performances. In order to gauge the responses from the creative team and the audiences, I plan to have discussions after the conclusion of the performance runs with these two groups. With the creative team, I will have one-on-one meetings to discuss their respective intended goals with the project and subse-

quent experiences; I will structure a set of conversational points to collect this anecdotal data. With audiences, I plan to send an online survey to their emails, as gathered through their registration for the event, to gauge their responses to the production.

Polling an audience seems like a logical conclusion to a project, but based on what Garrett said in his interview, I am inclined to read it as an example of academic drag where he wrote himself into a discourse to get something in return: money. To get that money, he needed to make his project "seem academic." In the interview, he said:

> Even in theater-based practice, when you're dealing with academic things, we have to somehow make it seem academic when it isn't always. I mean, it's the basic motions. I'm not going to do this, but I remember talking about the methodology and I'm like 'I'm going to do audience responses,' but that doesn't do shit to be quite honest. I might ask a couple. I might do that, but I think a survey's useless…I think I had to tweak my voice in order to accommodate getting money…if I want to get funding for my work, then this is what I have to do.

Later, as we were discussing the topic of agency, Garrett returned to the grant proposal, saying that even though it wasn't his voice, "I still feel like there was agency in that writing." The agency might be in how academic drag can be a resource for resistance insofar as it depends on metaknowledge of academic normativity and demonstrates a rhetorical savvy that highlights an intimate awareness of context with an ability to manipulate discourses at one's disposal. For Garrett, normative academic discourses were an obstacle to overcome to allow his more subversive artistic work to thrive,and it was through his donning of them—his attempts to "seem academic" despite feeling he was just going through the "basic motions"—that he was able to do work that was politically resistant in more visible and obvious ways.

Students as Analysts of their Own Rhetorical Context

In the examples we've discussed, we see students exercising an agency that constitutes resistance, although such resistance may not announce itself in clear and obvious ways. In a postcolonial context, students can and do echo back the language of their oppressors *in their writing* – but as historical researchers, this does not mean we can conclude that students *as political beings* supported the colonial project. Examining student writing with a wider lens – one that takes into account the pressures on students to assimilate into normativity, as well as *other* discourses that structured the teaching of writing in English, allows us to see other radical potentials in student writing while still speaking truth to power in quieter, smaller ways. The more recent examples show students engaging with normative discourses as a strategic choice to enable other types of political, artistic, or social resistance to flourish. To understand these examples as types of resistance—and thus to reclaim their rhetorical possibility under the framework of social justice—requires ways of reading that center student's contextual needs and embraces students as agentive analysts of their own rhetorical contexts

In Florianne's case, this means a triangulated approach to how she read student work: the close qualitative and rhetorical analysis of student writing needed to be placed into historical context through archival research. This triangulated approach was conscious of differences in power and agency between teachers and students, the colonizer and the colonized, and how these differences played out in the archives themselves. The absence of student voices and representations in the archives demonstrates the multiple levels of marginalization of her research subjects. To remedy this, Florianne deployed an archival method intended to reveal, on a macro scale (speeches, state reports, articles in national newspapers, political cartoons) and on a meso scale (administrative records, educational manuals, textbooks), the machinations of American colonial education. In her qualitative method, on the other hand, she analyzed Filipino student writing at an intensely micro level and examined dimensions of the texts such as teacher feedback and student revision, nationhood, and class and racial inequality. The process of reading widely in the archives, and then closely in the student writing, helped her understand student writing as shaped by and also shaping the discourses that happen outside of it. But to do this, she had to first immerse herself in the material conditions that Filipino students at the time were facing, and also be guided by the needs *they* articulated about writing, such as English langauge acquisition and socioeconomic mobility, and about colonial education. Methodologically, this requires centering student need by paying attention to the frames of knowing and understanding we apply to student writing as qualitative data.

In Joshua's case, in order to understand students' active analysis of their own rhetorical contexts, he needed to set aside his own desire to see students embrace anti-normative gestures and instead see rhetorical normativity as a strategic choice dependent on classroom context and larger student goals. One research participant, James, a senior Spanish and linguistics major, described how his feelings about what he wanted to write or talk about related to his sense of the classroom dynamic:

> I think unless you're writing in a setting where it's predominately or mostly queer people there's going to be a little bit of a moment of "Eww, I have to talk about this to straight people." In certain classes when we talk about queer issues the discussion is more like "Look, there, these people exist." And this sort of "they" conversation, almost as if there would never be any queer people in the room. Like, there are queer people in the room. I wouldn't say that I'm like horribly uncomfortable…it's just more the fact that if I'm going to talk about something queer, I'm going to have to say "we" where no one else is saying "we."

This act of risk assessment impacts how writers engage with the writing process—for example, whether writing would be peer reviewed by potentially hostile classmates was a particularly dominating factor in whether my research participants would choose to write about gender and/or sexuality, even when given the opportunity to do so by the teacher. As Blair, a trans student, put it, "Unless I trust my classmates to have Trans 101 knowledge, I will not write about gender." For Blair, protecting oneself from the potential harm from ignorant classmates—microaggressions in the classroom, or perhaps even macroaggressions that could affect them outside of it—was a more valuable strategic choice than educating them. On the other hand, someone like Garrett does want to resist gender and sexual norms and wants college to be a space for him to do this work. However, according to what he conveyed in his interview, he calculated that his college-level writing wasn't the place where that could effectively happen. Instead, he had to entangle with an audience that expected him to discuss his work in normatively academic ways, thus leading him to position his artistic project as a research process, downplaying the subversive, provocative nature of the piece.

What these examples from both Florianne and Joshua's research—from different time periods, different rhetorical contexts—show is a way of considering the normative (in the form of echoing, or in the form of academic drag) as one way marginalized students can deploy silence and normativity as rhetorical forms of resistance that, although perhaps not "critical-emancipatory," can nevertheless be imbued with a politics aimed toward justice and, at the very least, personal survival strategies. We see in these examples the calculated efforts of students who examine their rhetorical context and decide it's not safe or worth it to participate in academic discourses that might put them at harm or detract from their larger goals. In so doing, we encourage ways of reading students' texts that understand students might resist their teachers' good intentions through non-performance and deploy normative rhetorics for potentially subversive ends, conduits that students must engage with as they negotiate their own subjectivities, material circumstances, goals, and needs.

Conclusion

Both of us are compelled by many aspects of the social justice turn in the field. Our work, both as researchers and teachers, engages with marginalized student populations. We see our own narratives and experiences reflected in our students, and we also have individual political and personal investment in this turn. We think the social justice turn in the field is deeply necessary: Students need and deserve a better world, and we want to do our part, through our academic labor, to help create that world. However, we are also suspicious of the ways this academic labor has taken form. We want, both ourselves and the larger discipline, to proceed thoughtfully: How can we enact social justice for a better world, but not pre-determine what the better world is for our students? Can we step back and allow them to direct us there?

Our respective projects position students as acutely aware of these contexts, specifically the constraints, stakes, and implications of resistance and capitulation. This pushes against the fear-baiting discourse of *politicization* that is especially popular in conservative circles. The right wing sees college campuses as political battlegrounds, and college students as minds that must be cleared of "critical race theory." In this view, students become political *objects*. We instead choose to see students as political *actors* who are always-already political, even before we have encountered them in our classrooms. This is especially true for students whose identities, backgrounds, and personal contexts marginalize them.

However, we see the tendency of treating students as political objects in Writing Studies too, despite its seeming progressivism. Positioning teachers as the vanguard of the social justice turn denies the possibility that students could—in many ways do already—lead the way. That is to say, teacher-scholars might not be the people best equipped to teach resistance. In fact, our position in the student-teacher relationship needs to be interrogated, especially as we consider our research methods and pedagogy. As Kristofer Lotier bluntly pointed out in appraisal of critical pedagogy, "if instructors actually knew how to fix or overcome the complex problems of neoliberalism, no one would need to educate students to resist it; we would already be living in another world" (162-63).

The call to check ourselves and recenter students has emerged in some areas of the discipline. We are inspired by Sherri Craig's strident critique of contract grading practices: "Contract grading might make my colleagues feel good and ease the guilty burden of using practices with deep white supremacist origins in other areas of their courses, but it felt like a trap to me." In other words, when contract grading practices ask BIPOC students, who have been socialized for at least 12 years of traditional writing assessment to shift their views of the writing process, grading, and value, we re-center the teacher's view of how writing should be taught and valued to play savior. Similarly, we are drawn to Timothy Oleksiak's push against the unquestioned "improvement imperative" of peer review in the classroom. The grounding assumption behind this pedagogical commonplace is that students' texts aren't good enough as they are. This perspective, when deployed by teachers in a top-down fashion, is "shaped by an instructor's values regarding what counts as good writing" (309). In reframing how teacher-scholars notice and value resistance in our students, we build on these and other similar calls that ask for teacher-scholars to recognize and reimagine the power that they hold over students and student writing: no matter how much we believe in collaboration, dialogue, and equity with them, our students have been socialized in the normative, and potentially see us as part of normative structures. Arguably, they are correct in doing so since we do indeed work largely within the bounds of institutional contexts.

Writing Studies will continue to grow and change as the political realities shift. As part of that growth, we should consider what it means for students to engage in the work of social justice and our assumptions about what that looks like. As we strive to meet our ethical obligations to educate for social change, we may need to temper our pedagogy in light of emerging conceptions of what constitutes the counterhegemonic subject. While silence or conformity may indeed sometimes signal acceptance of a status quo, a writing economy of visibility and legibility, with "success" at social justice pedagogy being pre-prescribed, can be problematic and not attuned to the particularities of where students are writing from, in which contexts, and the role of academic discourse in those contexts. And in engaging with particularity, we should recognize the significance of understanding need from the student upward, not the instructor down. Perhaps that is the new work of social justice composition after all: to better listen to, and to find new ways to know, what students, in their various and specific contexts, are already telling us.

Works Cited

Alexander, Jonathan, and Jacqueline Rhodes. "Queer: An Impossible Subject for Composition." *JAC*, vol. 31, no. 1/2, 2011, pp. 177-206.

Bahri, Deepika. "Terms of Engagement: Postcolonialism, Transnationalism, and Composition Studies." *Crossing Borderlands: Composition and Postcolonial Studies,* edited by Andrea A. Lunsford and Lahoucine Ouzgane, U of Pittsburgh P, 2004, pp. 67-83.

Balce, Nerissa. *Body Parts of Empire : Visual Abjection, Filipino Images, and the American Archive / Nerissa Balce.* University of Michigan Press, 2016.

Banks, William P. "Written through the Body: Disruptions and 'Personal' Writing." *College English,* vol. 66, no. 1, Sept. 2003, p. 21.

Barszczewski, Joshua. "A Queer Rhetorics Framework for Discourse-Based Interviews." *Composition Forum,* vol. 49, 2022, https://compositionforum.com/issue/49/queer-rhetorics.php.

Bhabha, Homi. "Of Mimicry and Man: The Ambivalence of Colonial Discourse." *October,* vol. 28, no. 2, 1984, pp. 125-33. *JSTOR.*

Bizzell, Patricia. "Composition Studies Saves the World!" *College English,* vol. 72, no. 2, 2009, pp. 174-87.

Boyd, Richard. "Reading Student Resistance: The Case of the Missing Other." *JAC,* vol. 19, no. 4, 1999, pp. 589-605.

Carter, Shannon, Deborah Mutnick, Stephen Parks, and Jessica Pauszek. "Introduction: 'What Does Democracy Look Like?'" *Writing Democracy: The Political Turn in and beyond the Trump Era,* edited by Shannon Carter, Deborah Mutnick, Stephen Parks, and Jessica Pauszek. Routledge, 2020, pp. 1-24.

Clegg, Geoffrey. "Sustainable Audiences/Renewable Products: Penn State's Student Farm, Business Writing, and Community Outreach." *Writing Democracy: The Political Turn in and beyond the Trump Era,* edited by Shannon Carter et al. Routledge, 2020, pp. 150-161.

Craig, Sherri. "Your Contract Grading Ain't It." *WPA: Writing Program Administration,* vol. 44, no. 3, 2021, pp. 145-46.

Glenn, Cheryl. *Unspoken: A Rhetoric of Silence.* Southern Illinois UP, 2004.

Gorzelsky, Gwen. "Working Boundaries: From Student Resistance to Student Agency." *College Composition and Communication,* vol. 61, no. 1, 2009, pp. 64-84.

Harrington, Dana, and Anne C. Wheeler. "Rethinking Student Resistance from a Developmental Perspective." *Pedagogy,* vol. 20, no. 1, Jan. 2020, pp. 101-14.

Jimenez, Florianne. "Echoing + Resistant Imagining: Filipino Student Writing Under American Colonial Rule." *Journal for the History of Rhetoric,* vol. 24, no. 1, 2021, pp. 39-53.

Kinney, Kelly, Thomas Girshin, and Barret Bowlin. "The Third Turn toward the Social: Nancy Welchy's Living Room, Tony Scott's Dangerous Writing, and Rhetoric and Composition's Turn toward Grassroots Political Activism." Review of *Living Room: Teaching Public Writing in a Privatized World,* by Nancy Welch, and *Dangerous Writing: Understanding the Political Economy of Composition,* by Tony Scott. *Composition Forum,* vol. 21, 2010, https://compositionforum.com/issue/21/third-turn-social.php.

Kopelson, Karen. "Rhetoric on the Edge of Cunning: Or, the Performance of Neutrality (Re)Considered as a Composition Pedagogy for Student Resistance." *College Composition and Communication,* vol. 55, no. 1, 2003, pp. 115-46.

—. "Rhetoric on the Edge of Cunning Revisited: Of Truth and Lies in an Extra Urgent Sense." *Pedagogy,* vol. 20, no. 1, 2020, pp. 13-20.

Kramer, Paul. *The Blood of Government: Race, Empire, the United States, & the Philippines.* U of North Carolina P, 2006

Liu, Pei-Hsun Emma, and Dan J. Tannacito. "Resistance by L2 Writers: The Role of Racial and Language Ideology in Imagined Community and Identity Investment." *Journal of Second Language Writing*, vol. 22, no. 4, Dec. 2013, pp. 355-73.

Lotier, Kristopher M. "On Not Following Freire." *Pedagogy*, vol. 17, no. 2, 2017, pp. 151-75.

Miller, Richard E. "The Arts of Complicity: Pragmatism and the Culture of Schooling." *College English*, vol. 61, no. 1, 1998, pp. 10-28.

Morris III, Charles E. "(Self-)Portrait of Prof. R.C.: A Retrospective." *Western Journal of Communication*, vol. 74, no. 1, 2010, pp. 4-42.

Mutnick, Deborah. "A Pedagogy for the Political Turn." *Writing Democracy: The Political Turn in and beyond the Trump Era*. Eds. Shannon Carter et al. Routledge, 2020, pp. 82-108.

Oleksiak, Timothy. "A Queer Praxis for Peer Review." *College Composition and Communication.* vol. 72, no. 2 , 2020, pp. 306-32.

Palmeri, Jason. "Disruptive Queer Narratives in Composition and Literacy Studies." *College English*, vol. 80, no. 5, 2018, pp. 471-86.

Prasad, Pritha, and Louis M. Maraj. "'I Am Not Your Teaching Moment': The Benevolent Gaslight and Epistemic Violence." *College Composition and Communication*, vol. 74, no. 2, 2022, pp. 322-51.

Pratt, Mary Louise. "Arts of the Contact Zone." *Profession*, 1991, pp. 33-40.

Pritchard, Eric Darnell. *Fashioning Lives: Black Queers and the Politics of Literacy.* Southern Illinois University Press, 2017.

Reda, Mary. *Between Speaking and Silence: A Study of Quiet Students*. SUNY P, 2009.

Rhodes, Jacqueline, and Jonathan Alexander. "Reimagining the Social Turn: New Work from the Field." *College English*, vol. 76, no. 6, 2014, pp. 481-87.

Rodriguez, Dylan. *Suspended Apocalypse : White Supremacy, Genocide, and the Filipino Condition /Dylan Rodríguez.* University of Minnesota Press, 2010.

Samek, Alyssa A., and Theresa A. Donofrio. "'Academic Drag' and the Performance of the Critical Personae: An Exchange on Sexuality, Politics, and Identity in the Academy." *Women's Studies in Communication*, vol. 36, no. 1, Feb. 2013, pp. 28-55.

Smilges, J. Logan. *Queer Silence: On Disability and Rhetorical Absence.* U of Minnesota P, 2022.

Villanueva, Victor, Jr. "Maybe a Colony: And Still Another Critique of the Comp Community." *JAC,* vol. 17, no. 2, 1997, pp 183-90.

Waite, Stacey. *Teaching Queer: Radical Possibilities for Writing and Knowing.* University of Pittsburgh P, 2017.

Winkler, Ingo, and Irma Rybnikova. "Student Resistance in the Classroom—Functional-instrumentalist, Critical-emancipatory and Critical-functional Conceptualisations." *Higher Education Quarterly*, vol. 73, no. 4, Oct. 2019, pp. 521-38.

JAEPL, Vol. 29, 2024

Mapping James Moffett: Formative Assessment and Common Core Standards for the Contemporary Language Arts Classroom

Jonathan Marine and Ruth Nathan

Abstract: *In this article, we argue for an expanded conception of language assessment based on the principles of James Moffett and centered on outfitting teachers with useful information with which to guide their practice and optimize student learning. Importantly, we begin the article by demonstrating that Moffett's interest in assessing language growth occurs much earlier than previously thought. Then, we sketch a composite view of Moffett's evolving views on assessment as drawn from works across the span of his career while also investigating the many thinkers who influenced his ideas in order to situate them in the historical and educational context from which they emerged. Next, we present a selection of his growth sequences in order to take up both the principles which undergird them and their potential value for pedagogical practice while also mapping them to Common Core Readiness Anchor Standards (CCRAS). Finally, we discuss the implications of Moffett's work for writing assessment, educational policy, and national assessment standards.*

> *"External testing is nor more necessary for learning in school than for learning out of school."*

> —James Moffett, *Detecting Growth in Language*, p. 1

Introduction

Put plainly, summative and standardized assessments do little to inform or change teaching practices and instruction and can negatively impact students' self-efficacy and motivation. While most assessment in the United States is *summative* in nature (see Kibble) and focused on measuring the *outcomes* of student learning for comparative purposes, much scholarship attests to the limited impacts of summative assessment on student performance and their motivation to learn (see Harlen et al; Koenka).

However, *formative* assessment, monitoring students' learning in order to provide feedback that can be used to improve teaching and learning (Bennett; Black & Wiliam), offers teachers an expanded conception of the purpose of assessment as well as the opportunity to measure and assess student writing proficiency and progress in order to modify instruction and maximize student learning and development. Research on formative assessment has demonstrated its positive impact on learning, and its potential impact on student learning and achievement as supported by effective formative assessment practices in the classroom (see, for example, Afflerbach et al.; Gormley & McDermott; Lapp and Fisher). Yet, as Rysdam and Johnson-Shull note in their 2016 article on reframing written response, "conversation about teacher response to student work has gotten short shrift in our scholarly discussions about writing instruction" (70).

Especially in the early grades, assessing students' writing for the purposes of formative feedback is an under-researched topic (Skar et al.). While some scholarship has, for example, tried to utilize student self-assessment in order to support teachers' efforts to formatively monitor and adjust curriculum and instruction (Rogers et al.), there is limited research that centers on designing formative writing assessment tools for use by classroom teachers. As a result of the underutilization of formative writing assessment and the underreported nature of young learners' writing assessment, there exists both a research gap and a practical-knowledge gap (Marsh). Teachers' enactment of formative writing assessment is simply not sufficiently covered by the research base. One potentially rich source of actionable, theoretically informed formative language and writing assessment is the work of James Moffett.

Moffett and Assessment

James Moffett was a ground-breaking thinker, teacher, author, and theorist of language learning who impacted the fields of English Education, Language Arts, and Composition and who had a lasting impact on the National Council of Teachers of English (NCTE), the National Writing Project (NWP), and the Assembly for Expanded Perspectives on Learning (AEPL). Moffett's career was spent advocating for an expanded perspective on the teaching of the language arts and writing that derived its authority not from mere tradition but from a well-informed modern understanding of the linguistic and cognitive development of learners (Blau). However, over the course of his career, Moffett also sought to incorporate principles of mindfulness, spirituality, and holistic education (Durst; Marine & Rogers). As a result of arguing for what was at the time a radically expanded conception of the teaching of language, in the later stages of his career Moffett was increasingly focused on educational assessment and policy (Warnock) because he believed that language learning was deeply interwoven into how we discern our sense of self, civic duty, and purpose and meaning in life.

Moffett's only complete work dedicated to assessment, *Detecting Growth in Language*, decried standardized testing, arguing that assessment should instead take place by teachers for teachers' and students' benefit. Offering a "what to look for" approach, Moffett described growth in all aspects of language use, from whole texts to vocabulary development, stance, sentence structures, and the use of meta-language (e.g., conjunctions, relative pronouns, transition words, punctuation, paragraphing) to tie statements together across sentences, paragraphs, and entire discourses. Encapsulated in twenty-six growth sequences which holistically describe growth in language use relative to the overall intent of a given speech act or text, *Detecting Growth* offers a broader view of what counts as assessable behavior and language use in the classroom in order to help teachers assess for themselves their students' growth in language.

Yet Moffett's attention to assessment and evaluation began much earlier than 1992 (the year *Detecting Growth* was published). Further still, the many thinkers and theories which influenced his ideas on assessment and evaluation have never really been taken up or explored by scholars. Accordingly, in this essay, we seek to first demystify some of the influences on Moffett's ideas about evaluation and map the network of resources from which to draw a composite understanding of his theories on assessment before discussing how the growth sequences in *Detecting Growth* might be of use to contemporary classroom teachers.

In the following, we begin by sketching Moffett's evolving views on assessment drawn from works across the span of his career while also investigating the many factors which influenced his ideas and beliefs. Then, we situate his growth sequences in relation to Common Core standards before discussing their implications for pedagogical practice. Finally, we consider the implications of his work for writing assessment and educational policy and especially for national assessment standards. This account of Moffett's views on assessment and their potential value for classroom teachers, to quote Moffett, is "meant to be utilized, not believed... [we] are after a strategic gain in concept" (Moffett, *Teaching the Universe*, 15).

A Complicated Career, A Complicated Life

James Moffett wrote more than ten books and thirty articles and book chapters over the span of a one-of-a-kind career during which he bucked academe in order to impact more directly the teaching of language which he saw as the epicenter of education. During his life, he made a wide variety of contributions to, and impacts on, many different movements and fields, including the 1966 Dartmouth conference (Dixon; Miller), the progressive education movement (Burgess et al.), the National Council for the Teachers of English (Spalding et al.), and language education in Australia (Sawyer 2010). As a result of these numerous and diffuse areas of impact, mapping Moffett's evolving ideas on assessment is as challenging as understanding the many diverse influences which shaped his work and thinking on assessment throughout his lifetime.

The basic timeline of his thoughts on assessment as found in his published works, however, runs rather linearly from his landmark paired 1966 publications, *Teaching the Universe of Discourse* and *Student-Centered Language Arts*, across the teaching guides for the four levels of his language learning curriculum, *Interaction*, in the 1970s, through the four editions of *Active Voice* in the 1980s, and ending in 1992 with his only publication dedicated to language assessment, *Detecting Growth*. In trying to codify and understand the arc of his career, scholars have noted how following the Kanawha County protests of *Interaction* in 1973, Moffett increasingly turned "away from the mainstream in the teaching of English" (Durst, 112) in order to focus not only on meditation, mindfulness, and spirituality, but also on assessment, policy, and society as enmeshed, implicated, and interanimating with one another (see Moffett, *Universal Schoolhouse*). Yet, what this progression and these accounts have never truly addressed is the central event upon which Moffett's ideas with regard to assessment hinged: his involvement in, and recusal from, an effort to catalog behavioral objectives for the U.S. Department of Education in 1969.

As Moffett shared in the second chapter of *Coming on Center* (1st edition), entitled "Misbehavioral Subjectives," in 1969, he convened for five days with other leaders in English education and administration in order to write behavioral objectives for the U.S. Department of Education's "Catalog of Representative Behavioral Objectives, Grades

9-12." After realizing that the principles on which the objectives were based were not only overly rigid, but unproductive and even potentially harmful to students, Moffett agreed with the session leaders to leave the group and write a response to be included in the report based on the initiative (eventually published in 1970 as Chapter Nine of *On Writing Behavioral Objectives for English*).[1]

In that response, in which he proclaimed that "we are being MacNamara-ed," Moffett trenchantly deconstructed the underlying premise of the effort; namely, to reduce the teaching and learning of English to *only* behaviors which are explicitly observable (116). Arguing that "insisting that desirable behaviors be observable… rules out a great deal of learning," Moffett movingly critiqued the construct of observational objectivity and the value of behavioral objectives and, in doing so, demonstrated how language learning is far too complex an enterprise to interrogate using only stimulus-response methodology, particularly across short time spans (111).

What is most interesting about this moment in time, besides Moffett committing a kind of professional *harai karai* in order to maintain his own integrity and commitment to the basic principles of learning in which he believed,[2] is that shortly after this incident, in 1973's second edition of *Student-Centered Language Arts and Reading, K-13,* Moffett first shared twenty-four of the twenty-six growth sequences which would comprise *Detecting Growth in Language*. We know of no other scholarship which has denoted the emergence, almost twenty years earlier than most accounts suggest, of Moffett's vision for assessing growth in language in this much earlier publication. And this discovery helps to bind the timeline of Moffett's career with respect to evaluation and assessment much more tightly to this early controversy. It was clearly in response to this incident in 1969 that Moffett decided to try and take on devising an actionable (not to mention, *measurable*) series of constructs with which to assess growth in the language arts. The fact that the growth sequences were also republished in the third edition of *Student-Centered Language Arts* in 1983, shortly after *Misbehavioral Subjectives* in 1981, lends further credence and proof to this new account of the emergence of Moffett's theories on language assessment.

To be clear, this is not to say that Moffett's response was the only factor influencing his ideas. To the contrary, one only has to review the plethora of scholarly citations in his central theory, articulated as early as 1968 in *Teaching the Universe of Discourse*, to understand the vast array of philosophers, scientists, and educators who influenced his professional and personal life.[3] His consideration of philosophers like Susan Langer furthered his belief in the basic and pervasive human need to symbolize and invent

---

1. https://eric.ed.gov/?id=ED072465

2. Moffet notes he was offered the Presidency of NCTE as an effort to assuage his critique.

3. Psychologists (e.g., Piaget, Babette Whipple, Vygotsky, Robert Ornstein, Howard Gardner, Wendell Johnson, Roger Brown), sociologists (e.g., Basil Bernstein), English educators (e.g., Walter Loban, Carolyn Fitchett), linguists (e.g., John Mellon, Francis Christensen, Peter Rosenbaum, Kellogg Hunt) the anthropologist, H.E. Harlow, educational researchers (e.g., Janet Emig, Donald Graves, Mia Shaughnesy, Sonda Pearl, Adela Karliner, James Britton, Nancy Martin), and cognitive neuroscientists (e.g., Ursula Bellugi).

meanings. While from George Herbert Mead he drew the belief that verbal experience is central to what one is able to think, an idea that is also central to the work of another developmental psychologist whom Moffett cites repeatedly: Lev Vygotsky. Vygotsky famously formulated the concept of ZPD, the Zone of Proximal Development, which represents the distance between what a student can do on their own and what they can accomplish with the support of someone more knowledgeable about the undertaking. In this way, Moffett was also influenced by Piaget, whose ideas contributed to Moffett's theories of abstraction. Piaget's vast experimental work encouraged Moffett's understanding of development as incurred through the slow decentering of one's ego; of being able to see alternative perspectives, of standing in others' shoes.[4]

It is precisely these influences, along with the adjacent material in Moffett's oeuvre, which positions his work in *Detecting Growth* to serve teachers in the classroom interested in language assessment. For Moffett's growth sequences are not just evaluative categories but in fact an entire series of pedagogical principles which can be found interwoven into not only his other theoretical work, but also undergirded by the many activities and assignments which he (and his many collaborators) devised across his career, particularly in *Interaction*. In fact, many of Moffett's assignments presuppose the types of growth in language which *Detecting* seeks to illuminate, making his program uniquely suited to classroom teachers not only interested in a broader view of what counts as assessable behavior and language, but also the types of classroom activities which can support and promote the same types of growth which Moffett's sequences seek to measure.

Moffett's Growth Sequences

"This book is meant to help K-12 teachers assess verbal learning without external tests, by their own observations of learner activities and products" reads the first sentence of *Detecting Growth* (vii). It's a potent encapsulation of the premises undergirding Moffett's work in the book; namely, that assessment or evaluation is (or should be) *internal* to the classroom and based on the *observations* of teachers as they watch students perform language *naturally* as part of their everyday classroom activities. Compare this vision of assessment to the other state and national assessments which dominate education at the moment (like Virginia's SOL, or Maine's MEA, the New York's Regents Exam, or Texas's STAAR); rooms full of students quietly, individually filling out standardized, routinized examinations and never once talking or interacting with one another. This isn't to say these types of exams don't have a place or a purpose. It's merely meant to provoke a comparison to the lively, interactive, and kinetic world of classroom language use in which students actually live and learn and in doing so affirm the simple and undeniable fact that assessments which are not a part of everyday classroom activity *are not learning*; they are merely evaluations *of* the learning which has ostensibly *already* taken place. Moffett's proposal is delivered in his typical, casual "homespun style," (Blau) but the

---

4. For a more thorough account of Piaget's influence on Moffett, see "The Theoretical Genealogy of Steiner & Moffett," in *Toward a Re-Emergence of James Moffett's Mindful, Spiritual, and Student-Centered Pedagogy*, Peter Lang, 2023.

premise is even more revolutionary than when he first proposed it: learning and assessment should be one and the same.

Another element of Moffett's radical proposal in this book is the expanded range of 'languaging' behaviors which he believes should be accounted for in assessment. Most national or state-level standardized assessments rely heavily on writing for evaluation. However, Moffett convincingly situates writing as only one element in the spectrum of language arts, much as it is only one way in which we display or demonstrate our knowledge, learning, and growth. And this (what might be called) 'standardized myopia' is why Moffett believes it is vital language arts teachers learn to "detect growth constantly as they witness students discussing or performing, read or hear their writing, watch or listen to their tapes, listen in on or sit in with groups, confer with individuals, and register individuals' patterns of choice in their activities, materials, and partners" (*Detecting*, vii). What Moffett tries to facilitate with his sequences, then, are *ways of looking* for and at growth. The twenty-six sequences are presented as lenses through which to detect and think about the many different and idiosyncratic ways in which students grow, not directions or routines for how to perform assessment, not only because of the infinite array of ways in which growth might be detected, but also because Moffett "trusts teachers' experience and native perception" in a manner which external assessments endemically (and purposefully) seek to abrogate from the assessment process (vii).

This is all to say that, even before we look to Moffett's sequences for specific advice on detecting growth in language and the practical value they might hold for classroom teachers, it is important to acknowledge the drastically expanded perspective Moffett both offers and augurs insofar as how teachers might approach assessment. This shift in mindset is valuable on its own. In his critique, Moffet asserts that "national assessment exists to embarrass schools into improvement by comparing scores" (2). Conversely, for Moffett, assessment is *about* teachers, *for* teachers, and intended as a way to support learning, not weigh or compare schools, classes, or students against one another

Furthermore, Moffett reminds us that detecting growth in language is subtle work. Because thought is invisible to us until translated into acts or words, and since we can only see, read, or hear the language part, it's easy to forget the many processes which underlie its incarnation (6). There are a million contextual factors augmenting the process by which a thought or feeling manifests in language, and Moffett's main point is that we cannot, we must not, "just focus on language forms as if these existed alone" (6). The need to account for the entire spectrum of language arts *as* students learn is why he insists we situate assessment in the classrooms where learning is actually taking place and position it as a springboard to formatively adjust, individualize, and shape how teaching and learning transpires thereafter.

Growth Sequences #1–5

What perhaps delimits the uptake of Moffett's sequences is both the assumed knowledge of the system of thought and theory which undergirds them (and which is in some ways required to understand them) and the complexity of operationalizing them.[5] Take the first five sequences, for example:

1. Toward generalizing more broadly while elaborating more finely

2. Sending toward more general and more differentiated audiences

3. Toward increasing awareness that that people create what they know and that this knowledge is partial

4. Toward increasing awareness that meaning resides in minds, not in words, and that different people may see the same things differently, verbalize the same ideas differently, and interpret the same words differently

5. Toward increasingly sensitive judgment about when explicitness or implicitness is more appropriate in composing and comprehending.

There is a lot going on here. Sequence #1 revolves around the "dual function of abstracting"—namely, that we both abstract *from* the stimuli which abound our experiences, turning them *into* thoughts, compressing those thoughts into memory, and then, once a sufficient number of experiences collate with one another, fomenting generalizations, or rules and beliefs by which we then navigate and understand the world around us. But we also abstract *for*, parceling out a selection of that experiential data which we feel best fits our rhetorical purpose as we interact and communicate with others in a manner attuned to a given audience. But that complex, cognitive latticework only matters insofar as we are *aware* of these processes and are able to adjust that awareness to account for "differentiated audiences" (sequence #2), all of whom also undergo their own abstractive processes (sequence #3) and mean different things even when they say or use the same words (sequence #4), all of which has implications for how we shape and present our ideas (sequence #5). Having now gotten a sense of the intricacy at work in just the first few sequences, one is entitled to ask how any of this might benefit language arts teachers looking to detect growth in language in their own classrooms?

The answer lies in decreasing egocentrism (for which it again bears noting that Moffett relied heavily on Piaget and Vygotsky); the ability for our students to see the world through others' eyes, account for others' experiences, and leveraging that sensitivity and empathy to navigate how they communicate with their peers in order to garner the reactions they desire. Imagine, for example, a student telling a joke and expecting their audience to laugh or reading aloud a ghost story they've written and expecting their audience to cower in fear, or any one of a number of anticipated responses that accompany a student's act of speech or writing. It isn't to say that students should be able to garner the exact reaction they want with every communication they proffer so much as their ability to track those reactions and modify their discourse in real time based on the results.

---

5. It is important to acknowledge from the onset that a serious limitation of this article is that not all of Moffett's growth sequences and Common Core standards can be discussed here largely owing to space constraints. Instead, a select array of interesting, representative intersections will be examined as to provide what we hope is a promising jumping-off point for further inquiry.

This isn't simply audience awareness, either; it's also responsiveness and consideration of the experiences on which *their own perspectives* are based and the decentering of one's ego regarding how to express those experiences and the feelings and thoughts which emanate out of them in rhetorically savvy ways so as to achieve the reactions which they seek at any given moment from any given audience. A teacher who observes a student puzzled or frustrated by an audience response would do well to coach them through the kaleidoscopic perspectives governing the reception of their 'languaging,' much as the same teacher might benefit from tracking (read: detecting over time) how that student develops (read: growth) in subsequent exchanges of similar discourse. Of particular note in this regard is Moffett's suggestion to let students develop their own portfolios comprised of their work created over the course of an entire school year in order to allow both student and teacher to 'detect growth.'

Moffett's Growth Sequences and the CCRAS Standards for Reading

Moffett's Growth Sequences also align quite neatly with Common Core Readiness Anchor Standards (CCRAS). Take Growth Sequence #8 and CCRAS Reading Standard #1, for example (Table 1).

Table 1
Moffett's Growth Sequences and the CCRAS Standards for Reading

Moffett Growth Sequence #8	CCRAS Standard for Reading #1
Toward concepts of broader applicability, of larger membership, and of greater internal complexity of subclasses.	Read closely to determine what the text says explicitly and to make logical inferences from it; cite specific textual evidence when writing or speaking to support conclusions drawn from the text.

This CCRAS makes clear the need for highly specific vocabulary to both maintain cohesion and write in a formal style. And in Growth Sequence #8, Moffett demonstrates that vocabulary and concepts develop along the same trajectory as mental growth generally—toward broader generalization and finer elaboration. At first concepts are limited, as when a young child might refer to all water vessels as *boats*, but as writers (and readers) come to have experience with many types of boats, the particularity of a concept's subclass enhances communication by bringing specificity to the fore. Vocabulary and concept development is crucial for forming a cohesive argument, as it is for composing narrative, expository, and descriptive texts. From using appropriate synonyms to choosing words that reflect the desired tone given one's audience and purpose, the student writer benefits from a broad conceptual understanding. Let's take a look at some examples drawn from across different developmental periods:

> **Example - 3rd Grader:** Even though we are young, we can help out in the community. We could give ideas for making the city a better place for kids. (Kem-

per et al., 137) [note the specificity of the type of community being referred to: "the city"]

Example - Middle School Student: "I also dropped daphnia (brine shrimp) into the dish, and observed the way the hydra eats." (Kemper et al., 180) [note the desired tone given the use of "observed"]

Example - Adult: "The skull [from a T. Rex] will be sold in a live auction, a suitably old-school sendoff for a predator who bestrode the world 76 million years ago. But the skull which, which weighs 150-plus pounds and measures about 4 ½ feet long, seems much more than just an object. It isn't precisely a work of art, and Maximus was once alive. As someone with no interest in dinosaurs, I can't explain the appeal." (Cronin) [note how the desired tone is maintained with the choice of "bestrode" over "walked," for example]

Note not only how the conceptual borders widen as the writer ages in these examples, but also how much more complex the overlaying of subclasses becomes. A word like "community" may at first be daunting to taxonomize adeptly for a third grader, but as they learn and grow they come to place themselves, and the endless varieties of different *types* of "communities," in stark contrast to and with one another. By middle school, the writer knows that bringing up a specific type of shrimp begets a parenthetical explanation for their reader. And the adult writer in this example is interweaving all manner of subordinate and superordinate classes with one another: T. Rex, predator, skull, art; the writer is able to subtly communicate that the objects referred to in the writing exist in multiple classes and subclasses at once.

But it isn't just that Moffett's Growth Sequences align with CCRAS standards so much as the multiple growth sequences can be seen to cohere in specific CCRAS standards *at the same time*. Take Growth Sequences #18, #19, and #20 and the same CCRAS for Reading #1 (see Table 2).

All of these standards require the use of valid reasoning when reading and understanding arguments. The expansion of clause options as articulated in Growth Sequence #18 helps create cohesion, link major sections, and allow for varied syntax. To that end, Growth Sequences #19 and #20 add notions of versatility and expansion of rhetorical possibilities. As student growth continues from early elementary grades through high school, the language used to support "valid reasoning" requires the use, first, of linking words to connect opinions and arguments to reasons (Grades 1-4), but then quickly moves into the use of much more versatile words, phrases, and clauses by 5th grade.

In point of fact, the development of an argument (CCRAS Standard for Writing #1) requires an ever-expanding use of meta-language; language that encompasses the varied techniques writers use to join statements—from the use of pronouns, coordinating and subordinating conjunctions, and relative pronouns to transitional words, punctuation and paragraphing. Meta-language directs readers or listeners on how to take and relate statements. By expanding the repertory of clause-connecting options, by increasing versatility in constructing sentences, and by using and responding to the full rhetorical possibilities for tying ideas together, language users relate their analysis, reasoning, and evidence to one another, thereby logically enabling them to support an argument's claim. The rhetorical functions of these grammatical tools metamorphosize into an array of options for use in subtle communication through embedded meaning with important distinctions and modifications.

Table 2
Moffett's Growth Sequences and the CCRAS Standards for Reading

Moffett Growth Sequences #18, #19, #20	CCRAS Standard for Reading #1
Expanding the repertory of clause-connecting options as follows: String of separate independent clauses, each a sentence. Clauses conjoined by coordinating conjunctions (and, but, or) and time-apace conjunctions Clauses conjoined by logical subordinating conjunctions and fused by relative pronouns Clauses reduced and embedded in each other.	Read closely to determine what the text says explicitly and to make logical inferences from it; cite specific textual evidence when writing or speaking to support conclusions drawn from the text.
Toward increasing versatility in constructing sentences, exploiting more nearly the total resources inherent in modifying, conjoining, reducing, and embedding clauses; and toward increasing comprehension of sentences of such range.	
Toward and responding to the full rhetorical possibilities for chaining statements by grammar, transitional words, punctuation, paragraphing, and organizational form according to the commitment of the whole discourse.	

Moffett's Growth Sequences and the CCRAS Standards for Writing

Moffett's Growth Sequences also align with CCR standards for Writing as well. Take a look at Growth Sequence #18, 2, and 3 and CCR Standard for Writing #4, for example (Table 2).

Table 3

Moffett's Growth Sequences and the CCRAS Standards for Writing

Moffett Growth Sequence #18, 2, and 3	CCRAS for Writing
Growth Sequence # 18: Expanding the repertory of clause-connecting options as follows: A. String of separate independent clauses, each a sentence B. Clauses conjoined by coordinating conjunctions (and, but, or) and time-space conjunctions C. Clauses conjoined by logical subordinating conjunctions and fused by relative pronouns D. Clauses reduced and embedded in each other. #2: Sending toward more general and more differentiated audiences. #3: Toward increasing awareness that people create what they know and that this knowledge is partial.	Writing #4: Produce clear and coherent writing in which the development, organization, and style are appropriate to task, purpose, and audience.

The CCRAS for Writing #4 asks for "clear and coherent writing" and points toward growth in using transitional and connective devices, punctuation, paragraphing, parallel structure, repetition, and so on. Similarly, Moffett's Growth Sequence #18 calls teacher's attention to "expanding the repertory of clause-connecting" options, including stringing independent clauses together, coordinating conjunctions, subordinating conjunctions fused by relative pronouns, and embedded clauses. Viewed in this way, every sentence is a story unto itself, leaving readers the task of understanding what the writer is saying and seeing the relationships between ideas in order to understand the broader topic or story. The writer's task is to guide the reader through the many important interrelationships found across their ideas by utilizing an array of different connective devices which signal varying logical, temporal, and hierarchical relations.

Coherent writing requires sentences (whether one clause or many) to relate to one another according to the context of the whole discourse. As clauses are conjoined or embedded, they require certain meta-communicative words—conjunctions such as *but, or, although, because, unless,* and relative pronouns like *who, which,* and *where,* or conjunctive adverbs like *then, now, therefore, for example,* and *likewise.* As Moffett astutely suggests, "the statements *are* the communication, and these connectors meta-communicate about how to take and relate the sentences" (Moffett, *Detecting* 48-49). In order to demonstrate some of these connections in action, let's take a look at the work of a former 3rd grade student in one of Dr. Nathan's classes who we will call Lizzy:

The Roly Polies by Lizzy

When I first saw roly polies, I was two. They lived in a bush with dirt and flowers. They crawled all over me, but they didn't sting me. So, I've like roly polies since I was two!

Most people think roly polies are insects, but they're not. They're crustaceans. They are similar to insects because they have three body parts. They both have antennas and they both hatch eggs. They are not similar to insects because they have seven pairs of legs instead of six pairs.

Roly polies start their lives as eggs. Then they become mancas [pillbugs] and finally change into adults. Mancas [pillbugs] must molt to grow. They shed exoskeletons that cover their bodies.

As I said, roly polies get around on seven pairs of legs. Some rolly polies dig holes underground in soil. roly polies need to avoid the heat and come out at night. Their bodies dry out quickly. They roll up to keep moisture inside their bodies. They search for moist places to rest period.

Just like insects, roly polies have to eat. They enjoy eating rotting wood and dead animals, plants, and dead plants. Sometimes they eat other roly polies. When they eat, they do it with their mandibles. They use their strong moving parts to break down dead plants and leaves when they eat.

Some insects are friends and some are pests. Roly polies are nice. They don't bite. That makes them good for kids. For example, they roll in your hand, and when you put them down, they come unrolled. They are fun to watch and play with. In some ways they're pests because they can eat live plants. When the plants are in my mom's favorite flower bush or vegetables, it's bad.

It was fun writing this report. Now I have a new life skill. I wanted to study Roly polies because I've always loved to play with them. Now I understand why they act the way they do.

We see here that Lizzy is far beyond simply stringing independent clauses together. She has learned to meta-communicate—to relate statements to help her readers understand her complex ideas. The use of "As I said," in the sentence "As I said, roly polies get around on seven pairs of legs," reminds the reader that she's said this previously and signals that she is including additional context and clarification. Conversely, the use of "Just" in her sentence, "Just like insects, roly polies have to eat," shows degree. It functions as a cohesive device by indicating similarity and helps connect the idea of roly polies needing to eat with the concept of insects having the same need. Cohesive devices like this aid in the flow and organization of Lizzy's ideas and communicate to the reader that there is a shared characteristic between the two groups and are representative examples of the type of languaging ability which Moffett describes in growth sequence eighteen.

Similarly, the adverbial phrase, "for example" in the sentence, "For example, they roll in your hand, and when you put them down, they come unrolled," serves as a signal that the following information will provide a specific instance or illustration of the previous statement. "Now," in the sentence "Now I understand why they act the way they do," functions as an adverb that indicates a change in Lizzy's understanding or perception. She has gained insight (perhaps as she wrote her research report?) about why roly polies act the way they do; her "new life skill" has led to new revelations which she is in turn trying to communicate to her reader.

All of these connecting devices help Lizzy to transition more smoothly between her ideas and enhance the overall coherence of her sentences. They also help to demonstrate how Moffett's growth sequences align with CCRAS. And most importantly they showcase how a teacher might, over time, detect a student's growth in language as they utilize increasingly complex languaging skills. It is important to again note that Moffett's growth sequences are undergirded by one of the only fully developed theoretical models of first language learning (*Teaching the Universe of Discourse*, 1968) and connected to a host of activities, lessons, and pedagogical practices (*Student-Centered Language Arts*, 1968, 1976, 1983, 1991); few assessment standards contain the pedagogical theory and resources which Moffett's work offers.

By exploring Moffett's Growth Sequences and their compatibility with Common Core Readiness Anchor Standards, we also hope to underscore the significance of careful close reading in identifying language development. The more teachers are aware of these signs of growth, the better equipped they are to notice and name them for children. That the CCRAS can be seen as inclusive of such dexterous and sophisticated meaning making through language demonstrates quite strikingly how Moffett's growth sequences may be an important but little-known assessment *and* pedagogical tool with which to approach classroom language learning in ways that align with the state standards that many teachers are charged with accounting for in their classroom practices.

Conclusion

What does all of this mean for contemporary educators seeking an expanded perspective on language learning assessment and evaluation? First, it means that there is a startling complexity to be found in state standards often perceived as intrusive to and cloistering of pedagogical practice. State standards are intended as conceptual guidelines, even if they are sometimes wielded as constraints, and there remains room within each standard to approach growth in language holistically. Secondly, the work of James Moffett, and especially his militant reaction to the onset of the behavioral standards in the 1960s and 70s (which, not incidentally, may be seen as a forebearer of modern CCRAS) contains special value for language arts teachers tasked with managing classroom learning *and* standardized assessment benchmarks. That one of the most visionary and iconoclastic minds in language learning turned his attention to assessment, not only at the end but throughout his career, and the paucity of attention which that work has garnered, is an opportunity to re-attend to Moffett's nuanced and sophisticated ideas about language learning and especially his thoughts about *detecting growth in language.*

Of course, this article can only scrape the surface of that potential. There is simply too much going on in Moffett's twenty-six Growth Sequences (nine of which were reviewed in this essay) to summarily encapsulate the scope of this work. To that end, we have provided three appendices which attempt to chart many more of the CCRAS (for writing, reading, as well as speaking, listening and language) in conjunction with Moffett's growth sequences. Undoubtedly, further research on these sequences and their development over Moffett's career would unveil valuable insights which might further their potential use and applicability in concert with state standards in contemporary classrooms. That his works, including *Detecting Growth in Language*, have been recently made available in open access through the WAC Clearinghouse only adds to the urgency, and accessibility, of this endeavor.[6]

Moffett spent a great deal of time contemplating the unique demands of language on learners and especially for young learners. As he put it:

> [L]earners need to know that they can respond to mixed signals at once and don't have to select only one to respond to… [yet] only awareness and a larger perspective will permit them to make some whole in their minds of the mixed signals. Then they can respond to the whole at once. (*Detecting*, 31–32).

In the same way, as teachers of writing we must respond to the *whole student at once* by wading through the ambiguity of the individualized and often idiosyncratic growth of our students and attending to the uncanny variety of ways in which their language abilities might grow. In this way, Moffett's growth sequences serve as a powerful guide; a North Star in a storm of standardization and bureaucracy (Marine & Rogers). Assessment, as Moffett argued, exists (or should exist) *for the teacher*. Viewed in this way, assessment becomes a tool with which to better understand how to *work with students* to promote growth and learning. But to do so, we must first account for students in the assessment process, for as Moffett noted, "as soon as others want the results of learning more than the learner, the game is over" (*Detecting*, 27).

Works Cited

Afflerbach, Peter, Cho, Byeong-Young, and Kim, Jong-Yun. "Best Practices in Reading Assessment." *Best Practices in Literacy Instruction,* 2018, pp. 337-359.

Bennett, Randy Elliot. "Formative Assessment: A Critical Review." *Assessment in Education: Principles, Policy & Practice*, vol. 18, no. 1, 2011, pp. 5-25.

---

6. https://wac.colostate.edu/books/landmarks/moffett/

Black, Paul, and Dylan Wiliam. "Assessment and Classroom Learning." *Assessment in Education: Principles, Policy & Practice*, vol. 5, no. 1, 1998, pp. 7-74.

Blau, Sheridan. "Theory for Practice: James Moffett's Seminal Contribution to Composition." *Composition's Roots in English Education*, edited by P. Lambert Stock, Boynton Cook Publishers, 2011, pp. 81-104.

Burgess, Tony, Viv Ellis, and Sarah Roberts. "'How One Learns to Discourse': Writing and Abstraction in the Work of James Moffett and James Britton." *Changing English*, vol. 17, no. 3, 2010, pp. 261-274.

Cronin, Brenda. "Opinion | the 76-Million-Year-Old up for Adoption." *Wall Street Journal*, www.wsj.com/articles/the-76-million-year-old-up-for-adoption-maximus-t-rex-sothebys-auction-dinosaur-new-york-city-art-south-dakota-11669567903

Dixon, John. *Growth Through English: A Report Based on the Dartmouth Seminar*, 1966. United Kingdom, National Association for the Teaching of English, 1969.

Durst, Russel K. "The Stormy Times of James Moffett." *English Education*, vol. 47, no. 2, 2015, pp. 111-130.

Harlen, Wynne, Crick, Ruth D., Broadfoot, Patricia, Daugherty, Richard, Gardner, John, James, Mary, and Stobart, Gordon. "A Systematic Review of the Impact of Summative Assessment and Tests on Students' Motivation for Learning." *Evidence for Policy and Practice: Assessment and Learning Research Synthesis Group*, 2002.

Kemper, Dave. and Nathan, Ruth, and Sebranek, Patrick. *Write in Track: A Handbook for Young Writers Thinkers, and Learners*. Write Source/Houghton Mifflin, 1996.

Kemper, Dave, Sebranek, Patrick, and Verne Meyer, *All Write: A Student Handbook for Language and Learning*. Thoughtful Learning, 2016.

Kibble, Jonathan D. "Best Practices in Summative Assessment." *Advances in Physiology Education*, vol. 41, no. 1, 2017, pp. 110-119.

Koenka, Alison C. "Grade Expectations: The Motivational Consequences of Performance Feedback on a Summative Assessment." *The Journal of Experimental Education*, vol. 90, no. 1, 2022, pp. 88-111.

Lapp, Diane, and Douglas Fisher, eds. *Handbook of Research on Teaching the English Language Arts*. New York, NY: Routledge, 2011.

Marine, Jonathan, and Rogers, Paul. "Moffett's Turn to the Spiritual and Meditative." In *Toward a Re-Emergence of James Moffett's Mindful, Spiritual, and Student-Centered Pedagogy*, edited by Marine, Jonathan, Rogers, Paul, Blau, Sheridan, and Kelly, Kathleen. Peter Lang Publishing, 2023, pp. 1-24.

Marine, Jonathan. "The Theoretical Genealogy of Steiner & Moffett." In *Toward a Re-Emergence of James Moffett's Mindful, Spiritual, and Student-Centered Pedagogy*, edited by Marine, Jonathan, Rogers, Paul, Blau, Sheridan, and Kelly, Kathleen. Peter Lang Publishing, 2023, pp. 133-150.

Marsh, Colin J. "A Critical Analysis of the Use of Formative Assessment in Schools." *Educational Research for Policy and Practice*, vol. 6, no. 1, 2007, pp. 25-29.

McDermott, Peter, and Kathleen A. Gormley. "Teachers' Use of Technology in Elementary Reading Lessons." *Reading Psychology*, vol. 37, no. 1, 2016, pp. 121-146.

Moffett, James. *Teaching the Universe of Discourse*. Houghton Mifflin, 1968.

—. *A Student Centered Language Arts Curriculum, Grades K-13*. Houghton Mifflin, 1968.

—. "A Student-Centered Language Arts Curriculum: Grades K-13." Houghton Mifflin, 1973 Impression.

—. *Interaction: A Student Centered Language Arts and Reading Program.* Houghton Mifflin, 1973.

—. *Active Voice: A Writing Program across the Curriculum.* Boynton/Cook Publishers, Inc., 1981.

—. *Student Centered Language Arts, Grades K-12,* 4th Edition, Heinemann, 1991.

—. *Detecting Growth in Language.* Boynton/Cook Publishing, Inc., 1992.

Moffett, James and Tashlik, P., editors. *Active Voices II: Rationale and Teaching Guide: A Writer's Reader for Grades 7-9.* Boynton/Cook Publishers, Inc., 1986.

Moffett, J., Cooper, C., and Baker, M., editors. *Active Voices IV: A Writer's Reader.* Boynton/Cook Publishers, Inc., 1986.

Moffett, James, Wixon, Patty, Blau, Sheridan, and Phreaner, John, editors. *Active Voices III: A Writer's Readers: Grades 10-12.* Boynton/Cook Publishers, Inc., 1987.

Moffett, James and Wagner, B.J. *Student Centered Language Arts and Reading, Grades K-13,* 2nd Edition, Houghton Mifflin, 1976.

Moffett, James and Wagner, B.J. *Student-Centered Language Arts and Reading, Grades K-13,* 3rd Edition, Houghton Mifflin, 1983.

Muller, Herbert. *The Uses of English: Guidelines for the Teaching of English from the Anglo-American Conference at Dartmouth College.* New York, 1967.

Rogers, Paul M., Marine, Jonathan M., Ives, Samantha T., Parsons, Seth A., Horton, Ashley, and Young, Chase. "Validity Evidence for a Formative Writing Engagement Assessment in Elementary Grades." *Assessment in Education: Principles, Policy & Practice,* 2022, pp. 1-23.

Rysdam, Sheri, and Lisa Johnson-Shull. "Introducing Feedforward: Renaming and Reframing Our Repertoire for Written Response." *The Journal of the Assembly for Expanded Perspectives on Learning,* vol. 21, no. 1, 2016, pp. 69-85.

Sawyer, Wayne. "Structuring the New English in Australia: James Moffett and English Teaching in New South Wales." *Changing English,* vol. 17, no. 3, 2010, pp. 285-296.

Skar, Gustaf B., Steve Graham, and Gert Rijlaarsdam. "Formative Writing Assessment for Change." *Assessment in Education: Principles, Policy & Practice,* vol. 29, no. 2, 2022, pp. 121-126.

Spalding, Elizabeth, Damian C. Koshnick, and Miles Myers. "James Moffett's Legacy to English Journal." *English Journal,* vol. 101, no. 3, 2012, pp. 26-33.

Warnock, John. "James Moffett." *Twentieth Century Rhetorics and Rhetoricians: Critical Studies and Sources,* edited by M. G. Moran & M. Ballif. *Greenwood Press,* 2000, pp. 258-265.

Appendix A – CCR Reading Standards and Moffett's Growth Sequences

Common Core Anchor Standards for Reading	Moffett Growth Sequence Number(s)
1. Read closely to determine what the text says explicitly and to make logical inferences from it; cite specific textual evidence when writing or speaking to support conclusions drawn from the text.	1. 5, 7, 8, 13, 15
2. Determine central ideas or themes of a text and analyze their development; summarize the key supporting details and ideas.	1, 5, 7
3. Analyze how and why individuals, events, and ideas develop and interact over the course of a text.	2, 3, 4
4. Interpret words and phrases as they are used in a text, including determining technical, connotative, and figurative meanings, and analyze how specific word choices shape meaning or tone.	3, 4, 5, 7, 8, 9, 13, 16, 24
5. Analyze the structure of texts, including how specific sentences, paragraphs, and larger portions of the text (e.g., a section, chapter, scene, or stanza) relate to each other and the whole	13, 18, 19, 20
6. Assess how point of view or purpose shapes the content and style of a text.	3, 4, 6, 7
7. Integrate and evaluate content presented in diverse media and formats, including visually and quantitatively, as well as in words.	1, 3, 4

Common Core Anchor Standards for Reading	Moffett Growth Sequence Number(s)
8. Delineate and evaluate the argument and specific claims in a text, including the validity of the reasoning as well as the relevance and sufficiency of the evidence.	3, 4, 5, 26
9. Analyze how two or more texts address similar themes or topics in order to build knowledge or to compare the approaches the authors take.	3, 4, 18, 19, 26
10. Read and comprehend complex literary and informational texts independently and proficiently.	4, 23, 24, 25

Appendix B – CCR Writing Standards and Moffett's Growth Sequences

Common Core Anchor Standards for Writing	Moffett Growth Sequence Number(s)
1. Write arguments to support claims in an analysis of substantive topics or texts, using valid reasoning and relevant and sufficient evidence.	1, 2, 5, 6, 13, 17, 18, 19, 26
2. Write informative/explanatory texts to examine and convey complex ideas and information clearly and accurately through the effective selection, organization, and analysis of content.	1, 2, 5, 6, 13, 16, 17, 18, 19
3. Write narratives to develop real or imagined experiences or events using effective technique, well-chosen details, and well-structured event sequences.	1, 5, 13, 17, 24, 26

Common Core Anchor Standards for Writing	Moffett Growth Sequence Number(s)
4. Produce clear and coherent writing in which the development, organization, and style are appropriate to task, purpose, and audience.	1, 2, 3, 4, 5, 6,13, 16, 18, 19, 26
5. Develop and strengthen writing as needed by planning, revising, editing, rewriting, or trying a new approach.	1, 2, 5, 6, 13, 16, 18, 19, 26
6. Use technology, including the Internet, to produce and publish writing and to interact and collaborate with others.	2, 3, 4, 18, 26
7. Conduct short as well as more sustained research projects based on focused questions, demonstrating understanding of the subject under investigation.	8, 9, 10, 14, 23, 26
8. Gather relevant information from multiple print and digital sources, assess the credibility and accuracy of each source, and integrate the information while avoiding plagiarism.	3, 4, 6, 26
9. Draw evidence from literary and/or informational texts to support analysis, reflection, and research.	3, 6, 26
10. Write routinely over extended time frames (time for research, reflection, and revision) and shorter time frames (a single sitting or a day or two) for a range of tasks, purposes, and audiences.	2, 3, 4, 5, 6, 7

Appendix C – CCR Speaking and Listening Standards and Moffett's Growth Sequences

Common Core Anchor Standards for Speaking and Listening	Moffett Growth Sequence Number(s)
1. Prepare for and participate effectively in a range of conversations and collaborations with diverse partners, building on others' ideas and expressing their own clearly and persuasively.	4, 5, 6, 7, 9, 12, 13, 18, 19
2. Integrate and evaluate information presented in diverse media and formats, including visually, quantitatively, and orally.	3, 4, 5, 13
3. Evaluate a speaker's point of view, reasoning, and use of evidence and rhetoric.	3, 4, 5, 12, 20, 25
4. Present information, findings, and supporting evidence such that listeners can follow the line of reasoning and the organization, development, and style are appropriate to task, purpose, and audience.	3, 4, 5, 6, 12, 13, 14, 18, 19, 20, 23, 26
5. Make strategic use of digital media and visual displays of data to express information and enhance understanding of presentations.	2, 14, 18, 19, 26
6. Adapt speech to a variety of contexts and communicative tasks, demonstrating command of formal English when indicated or appropriate.	5, 6, 12, 13, 14, 18, 19, 23, 26

JAEPL, Vol. 29, 2024

CONNECTING

Creative Reading: Using Poetic Inquiry in Research and Teaching

Clancy Ratliff, with Abdullah-Al-Musayeb, Barja Islam, Mithila Mumtaz, Rosol Otear, Simon Richard, Noah Smith, Nuzhat Tarannum, and Allyssa Veney

All writing is autobiography.

—Donald Murray

I likely would not have experimented with poetic inquiry if I hadn't had two specific career experiences. The first was working with a graduate student whose thesis I was directing. His project argued for a genre-based approach to writing center tutoring. He proposed that writing centers keep repositories on-site of samples of many genres: grant proposals, cover letters, and more (still a good idea, I say). As I gave him feedback on chapter drafts, I reflected on the circulation of different genres of writing around me, and I realized that my mailbox is a genre box. Inspired by his genre repository idea, I decided to build my own genre repository. Close to a decade ago, I started saving what a lot of us call *junk mail*: mainly fundraising letters from nonprofit organizations, but also annual reports, push cards from electoral campaigns, legislative updates from congressional representatives, and legal dockets from advocacy groups with court cases pending. I receive at least a dozen pieces of mail a month from a variety of nonprofits on issues I care about: on feminism, civil liberties, fighting gun violence, addressing food insecurity, protecting animals, and climate action. I started collecting these genres, and I now have boxes of them. For years, I didn't know *what* I would do with them, but I was certain I would find a way to use them for my research.

The second of these career experiences was serving as co-editor of *Peitho*, the journal of the Coalition of Feminist Scholars in the History of Rhetoric and Composition. As I began the editing work, I read all the back issues of the journal, including many articles I hadn't read when those issues were first published. One of them was "From Resilience to Resistance: Repurposing Faculty Writers' Survival Strategies" by Sandra Tarabochia, which introduced me to poetic inquiry. Tarabochia interviewed faculty members about their writing practices and created data poems from the transcripts. A few months later, I realized: that's what I could do with the letters from nonprofits. I did more reading about poetic inquiry as a method, particularly work by Sandra Faulkner, including her book *Poetic Inquiry: Craft, Method and Practice*. My process of creating data poems from nonprofits' donor letters is similar to how Tarabochia describes composing her data poems:

> Because I was interested in exploring resilience, I paid particular attention to lines that captured adversity or faculty responses to adversity. I whittled down the file to the most poignant or impactful lines, the ones that provoked a bodily

reaction in me, and those that chillingly captured the essence of what I'd heard from other participants. Next, I grouped the lines that spoke to each other and chose lines to title those groups. Finally, I arranged the lines within each group into stanzas that addressed different aspects of the topic or communicated a feeling.

Through the process of poetic inquiry, Tarabochia arrives at a clearer understanding of what resilience means for faculty writers. She finds that resilience is constructed (based on narratives about adversity and resilience), nonlinear (not a clean progression from non-resilience to strong resilience), and discursive (situated in neoliberal discourses about academia).

Researching with Poetic Inquiry

This essay is a reflection on my ongoing foray into poetic inquiry, a relatively new method situated in arts-based research (ABR), and how we might use such methodology in the classroom with students to promote their creative relationship to language and help them learn about the everyday discourses they encounter. Poetic inquiry has been practiced for about twenty years, but it still isn't a widely recognized method that would, for example, be included in a seminar about research methods. Poetic inquiry is a process of creating data poems from a corpus of text, often from transcripts of interviews with research participants. There is poetic transcription, which hews closer to the original text in the corpus and retains its syntax, but poetic inquiry can also encompass taking more creative liberties with the text. Regardless of the approach, poetic inquiry should be both good research and good poetry. I think poetic inquiry can be used pedagogically as well. In a previous issue of *JAEPL*, Mariya Deykute argues for poetic inquiry's value for students who are studying sciences; she makes a persuasive case for teaching creative writing alongside and integrated with degree programs in the sciences. Deykute observes that "The pathetic appeal of poetry is not, contrary to how it may be perceived, a weakness and should not be excluded from our understanding of science and its communication…learning is enhanced when the content is connected to the emotional human core of the learner and that the objectivity of scientific communication or thought can benefit from consideration of the emotional core forming human associations with facts and discoveries" (35). Poetry connects. The focus of my essay is sharing my own journey with poetic inquiry, the data poems that my students and I have composed, and why I think poetic inquiry can be a powerful tool for engaging with texts.

I have written about using poetic inquiry to study abortion rights rhetoric, including data poems from letters by feminist nonprofits (Ratliff, "'We Won't Back Down'"), and I'm working on a larger project using poetic inquiry to analyze the environmental rhetoric in letters from environmentalist advocacy organizations. The data poems I'm sharing here are my first efforts, when I was practicing the method. What follows are two of my data poems: one on hunger and food insecurity using letters from food aid nonprofits, and one on veterans and the issues they face using letters from veterans' advocacy organizations. The original letters that serve as the source text for these data poems are included as an appendix.

The Hunger Poem (letters from Second Harvest South Louisiana, Christian Appalachian Project, and Catholic Charities of Acadiana)

Holidays should be a time of joy and plenty
no one in our community should go hungry
Unimaginable hardship and hopelessness
the need for food has skyrocketed
far too much for them to bear

This extremely difficult holiday season
feed children in South Louisiana.
Hurricanes Laura and Delta
Those who cannot rebound on their own
Those who suffer under the burden of multiple disasters

A can of beans, a loaf of bread, a bag of rice
pleading eyes of worried parents and their children
Anything to feed their little ones
Fill empty plates with nutritious food

Another holiday of historic hunger

The Veterans Poem (letters from the Wounded Warrior Project, Operation VetCare, and Veterans of Foreign Wars)

Wounded veterans who have returned from Iraq and Afghanistan can't wait
More than 413,800 military veterans have experienced a traumatic brain injury
Veterans who suffer in silence
A military family that's facing a crisis
The invisible wounds of war
Terrorized night and day by the horror of post-traumatic stress
You can't "see" the nightmares or sleeplessness

An improvised explosive device detonated
Third-degree burns
More than 70 painful surgeries
Months in a coma
Nerve damage

$11 million in emergency assistance
Make sure spouses and children receive the survivor benefits they need and deserve
Services in mental health, career counseling, and long-term rehabilitative care change lives

Many patients do not receive visitors
Help from kind friends brings relief and hope
Financial, emotional, and physical challenges
Make a home repair
Mow the grass
Simply stay and chat
We are honored to assist our wounded warriors

What my own experimentation with poetic inquiry has helped me understand is the creative potential in reading. I already understood the conventions of the donor letter genre: the typical formula is that the organization presents the current dire conditions, but they stop short of claiming that the situation is hopeless. They point to gains their organization has made and ways they have intervened: lawsuits, or helping people by providing food or other aid. They tell readers that their financial contributions make this work possible and urge them to donate. However, when I created data poems from the letters, I was able to read letters from multiple organizations focused on one cause (for example, reproductive justice) and think about the common themes. For abortion rights nonprofits, that included conditions at clinics, Supreme Court justices, and the Global Gag Rule, among other themes, and I was able to think creatively and generatively about combining phrases from across the letters into poems. I created a new interlocutor: the speaker of the data poem. The speaker of the poem is not I, Clancy Ratliff, or the writers of the letters, but a new textual persona. I arranged the phrases into lines and stanzas for aesthetic and emotional impact.

Teaching with Poetic Inquiry

Admittedly, I have only used poetic inquiry once so far in my teaching. Still, I think it has great potential to be an engaging activity to facilitate critical reading for students. Reading has regained the attention of rhetoric and composition scholars in recent years, with a 2021 position statement from the Conference on College Composition and Communication on the role of reading in college writing classes, a special issue of *Teaching English in the Two-Year College* on reading in open-access institutions, and a new book about the history of reading in writing studies (Horning). Poetic inquiry reading activities could be integrated into a writing class using an *I do, we do, you do* procedure: the instructor briefly introduces poetic inquiry and demonstrates creating a data poem from a previously assigned reading in the class, then the class reviews an assigned reading and creates a poem together, and finally, individual students do their own data poems from sections of an assigned reading. Howard Tinberg writes about a similar activity he has done in class: bringing one copy of Martin Luther King Jr.'s "Letter from Birmingham Jail" to class, putting students in groups of three or four students each, and giving one or two pages of King's letter to each group. He asks students to read the page aloud and then answer the questions: "Which passages draw you 'in'? Which passages push you 'out'?" (229). Students then underline and annotate these passages on their page, discuss reasons they felt drawn in or pushed out, and then Tinberg has them share their findings with the class, from the first page to the last. Poetic inquiry would take this process a step further by assembling the passages into poems.

This semester, I am teaching a cross-listed undergraduate/graduate course in ancient rhetoric. As an in-class activity, I had students compose poems from Isocrates's "Against the Sophists." I first gave them some background about poetic inquiry and showed them some of my data poems, and then I asked them to take fifteen minutes and create a poem with phrases from "Against the Sophists," which was the reading for that day. I did the activity with them, and here is my poem:

They Are Sophists

> They say they have no need for money
> They pretend to know the future
> They have no concern for the truth
> They themselves are so senseless
> They have a poor understanding
> They promise to teach lawcourt skills
> They say that the science of speeches is like teaching the alphabet

I explained to students that I noticed the many "they" statements in Isocrates's text and figured I would try assembling them into a poem. I asked students to share their poems, clarifying that it was voluntary and they should only share if they were comfortable doing so. These are their data poems from "Against the Sophists":

If Only

by Mithila Mumtaz

> If only they had spoken the truth,
> If only they'd avoided ill repute,
> If only they would cease pretension—
> For no one knows the truth.
> Even gods, at times, are left in doubt,
> Yet they are bold,
> Persuading youth, the so-called 'old.'
> They promise them the lie—
> Money, the concern for which they cry.

Beneath the Letters

by Rosol Otear

> They say they don't care for riches,
> but they stretch their hands for gold.
> They offer wisdom, claim to know the way,
> but they know none
> They demand,

but do not practice what they preach
They speak of trust,
but distrust the very ones they mold?
They liken speech to letters learned,
but they know not that the truth lies beneath the letters?

Isocrates and the Sophists

by Noah Smith

Who would not hate and despise...those who spend their time in disputes,
Pretending to seek the truth but from the beginning of their lessons to lie,
They say they have no need for money,
And they deposit the fees from their students with men whom they have never taught,
I am amazed when I see these men claiming students for themselves,
using an ordered art as a model for creative activity -
Propriety and originality none of these requirements extend to letters -
They themselves need such instruction
I think it is reasonable to despise such pursuits, idle and trivial, not a cultivation of the soul

Unmasking the Sophists

by Barja Islam

Sophists promise wisdom, but are they aware?
They are teaching virtues while greed is showing the flare.
With hollow rhetoric, they lead us astray.
And impart grand knowledge in exchange for pay.
So let us reflect on what is right
And seek pure wisdom in the light,
For those who teach; must first be Just!
In virtue and wisdom, we place our trust.

On Against the Sophists

by Allyssa Veney

> Who can fail to abhor their attempts to deceive us?
> Not ashamed to hold their hands out to their disciples,
> They require the opposite of what they preach.
> Is it not absurd that they are blind to inconsistencies?
> The teacher must set an example not found in others.

The Masters of False Goods

by Abdullah-Al-Musayeb

> Their 'greater promises'
> are 'lessons to lie'.
> They 'persuade the young'
> that 'knowledge' brings happiness
> for just 'three or four minas'
> And thus become 'masters of great goods'.

Shadows of Sophists

by Nuzhat Tarannum

> Pedagogues who express veracity,
> Never express a loss of prosperity.
> Those who boast without care,
> Their wiser thoughts are not near.
> Those who deceive with argues and claims,
> Pretend the truth but tamper it in a frame.

Stolen Wisdom

by Simon Richard

> They say education is the only way,
> yet only want their money.
> They speak enough truth for us to listen,
> then shower us with lies.
> "You will be a failure without college."
> As if student debt doesn't exist
> Reform! Reform! Reform!

After we composed and shared these poems in class, I asked students if they had any impressions or questions about poetic inquiry. Their responses were interesting. One student had a question about how strict the guidelines are for creating data poems: do the lines in the poems have to be the exact words in the source text, or is there flexibility? I explained that poetic inquiry is as much about good poetry as it is about good research, and scholars who use it often make slight changes to wording, grammar, and syntax to make a data poem better, as long as the meaning is intact, and that lines in a data poem don't have to go in order of appearance in the source text. Another student observed that poetic inquiry is a way to approach the text in a more nonlinear way. He said that it was interesting to take phrases from toward the end of the text and put them at the beginning of a data poem (and phrases from the beginning of the source text at the end of the data poem) to see if the argument is different.

We remember Murray's concisely worded statement "all writing is autobiography," but at the close of that essay, he also says, "That is the terrible, wonderful power of reading: the texts we create in our own minds while we read—or just after we read—become part of the life we believe we lived. Another thesis: *all reading is autobiographical*" (74, my emphasis). The lifting and arrangement of phrases from a text provide a record of what resonates with a reader and how they receive and interpret a text, an accessible entry to the text that lets students set aside worries about misreading and misinterpreting. Students are accustomed to a few ways of demonstrating engagement with reading, or, to put it more bluntly, showing that they did the assigned reading. These include quizzes, short written responses, and speaking in class discussion. In each case, students may perceive a risk of saying the wrong thing about the reading, and understandably so; comprehending complex texts assigned in college courses can require considerable background knowledge about the historical and cultural context of the text and the author's other work. Creating a data poem about an assigned reading removes some of the pressure to interpret a text *correctly*, and it makes the text accessible to students who may not have the extensive knowledge base or life experience to encounter the reading with a command of its context. Poetic inquiry can give students a point of entry that we, as instructors, can build on to give them more confidence as readers, and the exercise of playing with language can enhance students' development as writers.

Works Cited

Conference on College Composition and Communication. "CCCC Position Statement on the Role of Reading in College Writing Classrooms." March 2021, cccc.ncte.org/cccc/the-role-of-reading. Accessed 14 Sept. 2024.

Deykute, Mariya. "All Scientists Should Write Poetry: Creative Writing as Essential Academic Practice." *Journal for the Assembly for Expanded Perspectives on Learning*, vol. 27, 2021-22, pp. 20-38.

Faulkner, Sandra. *Poetic Inquiry: Craft, Method, and Practice*. 2nd ed., Routledge, 2020.

Giordano, Joanne Baird, and Cheryl Hogue Smith, eds. *Teaching Reading in Open-Access Contexts*, special issue of *Teaching English in the Two-Year College*, vol. 50, no. 2, 2022, https://doi.org/10.58680/tetyc202232295.

Horning, Alice S. *The Case for Critical Literacy: The History of Reading in Writing Studies*. Utah State UP, 2024.

Murray, Donald M. "All Writing Is Autobiography." *College Composition and Communication*, vol 42, no. 1, 1991, pp. 66-74.

Ratliff, Clancy. "'We Won't Back Down: Feeling Abortion Rights Rhetoric through Poetic Inquiry." In *The Routledge Handbook of Contemporary Feminist Rhetoric*, edited by Jacqueline Rhodes and Suban Nur Cooley. Routledge, 2024, pp. 304-314.

Tinberg, Howard, and Matthew Davis. "Reading and the Teaching for Transfer (TFT) Curriculum." In *Deep Reading, Deep Learning*, Volume 2, edited by Patrick Sullivan, Sheridan Blau, and Howard Tinberg. Peter Lang, 2023, pp. 221-232.

Tarabochia, Sandra L. "From Resilience to Resistance: Repurposing Faculty Writers' Survival Strategies." *Peitho* vol. 23, no. 3, 2021, wac.colostate.edu/docs/peitho/article/from-resilience-to-resistance-repurposing-faculty-writers-survival-strategies/. Accessed 14 Sept. 2024.

Appendix

SECOND HARVEST
FOOD BANK
FEEDING SOUTH LOUISIANA

Second Harvest works in partnership with

AMERICA   NEW ORLEANS   United Way

Clancy Ratliff

PROJECT $0.00

||₁||₁·|₁₁|||₁₁₁ₐₗ·|₁₁ₑₚₐ|₁|₁ₑₗ·|ₐₚₗₑₗ||ₐₗₗ||||₁ₗₐₗₗ||ₗ||

**For $1, you can help
provide 4 meals for a hungry
person in our community
this Thanksgiving!**

Dear Mr. Ratliff,

Thanksgiving will be here before we know it. But extreme challenges this year means more of our neighbors than ever won't be able to afford a meal. Many are turning to Second Harvest Food Bank for the first time. Unemployment is still high. Many people are having to choose between paying for rent and utilities ... or buying food.

That's why Second Harvest partners with pantries, soup kitchens, shelters, and other hunger-relief organizations to make sure our neighbors have access to nutritious food this Thanksgiving — and throughout this difficult time.

Kathy and her husband have been struggling to get by on a single income ever since health concerns forced her out of work earlier this year. *"I'm doing everything I can to get back the life we had,"* Kathy said. *"But it's a scary feeling not having enough money to feed your kids. What happens to them if there's nowhere we can turn for food?"*

All across South Louisiana, the need for food has skyrocketed. And we're expecting thousands more children, families, and seniors will need our help before the year is over.

We believe no one in our community should go hungry, and we're committed to ensuring our neighbors have nutritious food to eat.

It takes a lot of support to feed so many people — but with your help, we can do it. Every dollar you give helps provide four meals for people in South Louisiana this Thanksgiving.

That means your gift of $10 sent along with two of the enclosed Thanksgiving Food Delivery Tickets will help provide 40 meals to a hungry neighbor.

Your gift of $15 with three tickets will help provide 60 meals! Or maybe you can find it in your heart to send a gift of $20 to help provide 80 meals.

Please help feed our hungry neighbors today. I can't tell you what it means to see the relief and gratitude on the faces of men, women, and children who receive a Thanksgiving meal they did not think they would have.

Every person makes a difference and every gift counts — so please give your best gift today. Together, we can fill empty plates with nutritious food this Thanksgiving and throughout the year.

Sincerely,

Natalie Jayroe
President and CEO

P.S.   Incredible hardship this year has led to incredible hunger in South Louisiana. Your gift is urgently needed to provide meals to the record-number of people struggling to put food on the table this Thanksgiving. Please give today!

SECOND HARVEST FOOD BANK
FEEDING SOUTH LOUISIANA
NEW ORLEANS   FEEDING AMERICA

Clancy Ratliff
PROJECT   16 98
||¦|¦|¦·||¦···||¦·¦|¦·¦||||||¦|¦|···||¦¦|·¦|¦|·|¦¦|¦¦|¦¦|¦¦|¦|¦|

For $1, you can help provide 4 meals to a person struggling with hunger in our community this Thanksgiving!

Dear Mr. Ratliff,

Thanksgiving will be here before we know it. However, ongoing hardship will mean a lot of our neighbors won't be able to afford a meal. Many of the people who lost their jobs and livelihoods last year are still recovering. Meanwhile, the high food costs are stretching their budgets even thinner, forcing many to choose between paying the bills … or buying food.

That's why Second Harvest Food Bank partners with pantries, soup kitchens, shelters, and other hunger-relief organizations to make sure our neighbors have access to nutritious food this Thanksgiving.

It's Rebecca's top priority to make sure her kids don't feel the impact of her and her husband's unemployment. For months, the young parents have been working multiple odd jobs, skipping meals, and making tough choices to keep food on the table. Because even if they can cover rent and utilities — there's not always enough for trips to the grocery store, too.

All across South Louisiana, the demand for food is high. And we're expecting thousands more will need help finding good food and meals before the year is over.

We believe no one in our community should go hungry, and we're committed to ensuring our neighbors have nutritious food to eat.

It takes a lot of support to feed so many people — but with your help, we can do it. **Every $1 you give helps provide enough food for 4 meals for people in South Louisiana this Thanksgiving.**

That means your gift of $10 sent along with two of the enclosed Thanksgiving Food Delivery Tickets will provide 40 meals to a hungry neighbor.

Your gift of $15 with three tickets will provide 60 meals! Or maybe you can find it in your heart to send a gift of $20 to provide 80 meals.

Please help feed our hungry neighbors today. I can't tell you what it means to see the relief and gratitude on the faces of men, women, and children who receive a Thanksgiving meal they did not think they would have.

Every person makes a difference and every gift counts — so please give your best gift today. Together, we can fill empty plates with nutritious food this Thanksgiving and throughout the year.

Sincerely,

Natalie

Natalie Jayroe
President and CEO

P.S.   This will be another holiday of historic hunger in South Louisiana. Please give today to provide meals to families struggling to put food on the table this Thanksgiving. To give online, please visit no-hunger.org/thanksgiving.

SECOND HARVEST FOOD BANK
FEEDING SOUTH LOUISIANA

Dear Mr. Ratliff,

I hope this letter finds you in peace and good health this holiday season. If you're like me, it's hard not to dwell on the many ways this season differs from years past.

But for all the uncertainty and change, there's something much worse being felt in our community right now. Hunger.

Job loss and hardship have led to record-levels of hunger in South Louisiana this year. Many of your neighbors are struggling to recover and can't afford to eat. Their health, and their children's health, are under threat.

> **That's why I'm asking you to please rush your generous contribution of $40 to help provide 160 meals … $50 to help provide 200 meals … or even $75 to help provide 300 meals to our neighbors facing hunger.**

In the holiday spirit of compassion and sharing, please give generously today. When you do, you'll give families who don't know where their next meal is coming from food to fill their plates, and one less worry during this extremely difficult holiday season.

Thank you so much for caring and giving!

Sincerely,

Natalie Jayroe
President and CEO

P.S.   **Please give today to provide food to struggling neighbors in their time of greatest need.** You can donate online at no-hunger.org.

SECOND HARVEST FOOD BANK
FEEDING SOUTH LOUISIANA

Dear Mr. Ratliff,

Holidays should be a time of joy and plenty. But for our hungry neighbors, the holidays make going without even more painful. The ever-increasing cost of groceries, utilities, and other basic needs are pushing hard-working families in South Louisiana beyond their means. They simply cannot provide for themselves and their families, even if they work two jobs.

For those struggling to make ends meet, there will be no beautiful decorations … no wrapped packages … no holiday meal shared with family and friends.

That's why I'm asking you to please rush your generous contribution of $40 to help provide 160 meals … $50 to help provide 200 meals … or even $100 to ensure 400 meals are fed to our hungriest neighbors this holiday season.

In the holiday spirit of compassion and sharing, <u>please send your gift today</u>. You'll give families who don't know where their next meal is coming from food to fill their plates, and one less worry this season.

Thank you so much for caring and giving!

Sincerely,

Natalie Jayroe
President and CEO

P.S. Please send your gift today. Your gift will put food on a hungry family's table. You can donate online at no-hunger.org.

```
1 in 4 children
in our community
is facing hunger
this summer.

You can change
this with a
gift today.
```

Dear Friend,

Did you know summer is the hungriest time of year for children and their families?

For kids relying on school-provided meals, summer was already a difficult time. Now, with so many families in crisis, this summer is even worse. Parents already struggling to get by don't know how they'll cover those meals this summer and more children are going hungry.

We need your help to feed children in South Louisiana who might otherwise go hungry this summer.

Last year, child hunger increased by more than 25% in South Louisiana due to the COVID-19 pandemic. We're expecting the high need to continue through the end of 2021.

Even though hunger and the need for food in our community remain at a heartbreaking high, we often experience a decline in donations this time of year. **That's why your gift is urgently needed today. Every $1 you donate can help provide 4 meals.**

With your donation and our resources, we can provide meals to children facing hunger all summer long. That's why I've included two vouchers. A gift in June and another in July will help for the entire season. Or, if you prefer, you can give one gift for the entire summer.

You can let hungry children in our community know you care with a gift to Second Harvest Food Bank. **Your generosity today will ensure that children and families have the food they need — all summer long.**

Thank you for caring.

Natalie Jayroe
President and CEO

P.S.   When school ends, so does access to nutritious meals for many children in our community. Please give today to provide meals to hungry children all summer long. If you'd like to make your gift online, visit no-hunger.org.

What will we do next month?

Please feed a child in need in Appalachia today.

Dear Friend,

I'm writing you this letter and praying that as you read it, God will fill your heart with compassion ... because I have never seen anything like this.

For months now, our food pantry manager has been looking into the pleading eyes of worried parents and their children — who are very hungry — as they stand in long lines, waiting for nourishing food ... and praying to God we will have enough food to feed them.

Our *Grateful Bread Food Pantry*, which was meant to feed 300 people each month, is overwhelmed by new families in need because of the pandemic.

Every day, we see long lines of moms, dads, and grandparents waiting their turn for a can of beans, a loaf of bread, a bag of rice — *just anything to feed their little ones* — and they pray this won't be the day we run out.

And I pray that we never see the day when we can't help people in need!

That's why you'll find four mini "meal tickets" attached to your reply form. Each one shows how your generous donation can make a life-changing impact.

Did you know that thanks to food and monetary donations, we can feed a child a healthy meal for just 59¢? Just imagine how many hungry children your generous gift can feed today!

It takes so little to do so much good.   *You can feed a child in need!*

Still, I know that not everyone who reads this letter will be able to donate. But I hope you are able to.

Can I count on you to help feed a hungry child and their family?

That is how Christian Appalachian Project began in 1964 — in the back of a small church, with just a small group of caring friends collecting canned goods, old clothing and

(over, please)

Christian Appalachian Project

485 Ponderosa Drive • PO Box 1768 • Paintsville, KY 41240 • 1-866-270-4CAP (4227) • ChristianApp.org

shoes, and whatever else they had to give to people in need.

During the holidays, food baskets were given out to feed children and families who were hungry and living in distressed homes in isolated areas.

Americans in most need — those living in isolation and suffering … our brothers and sisters who are elderly or sick … and people with disabilities — **can find a glimmer of hope to hang on to in Christian Appalachian Project.**

Today, Appalachia is a place where only the most fortunate have jobs, where once-thriving coal mines have long ago closed and manufacturing jobs have since moved overseas.

Seniors in Appalachia need your help.

Many families are barely surviving.

The Census Bureau recently called the central Appalachian states our nation's poorest, with extreme poverty at an all-time high. For people already battling incredible need, the aftermath of a pandemic — and the unemployment it caused — means unimaginable hardship and hopelessness.

No one should have to live in deplorable conditions. No child in America should be hungry — and find the kitchen cupboard is bare.

We see the tear-streaked faces and pleading eyes of little children … the thin, drawn hands of the elderly … and mothers clutching babies who are weakened by hunger.

And that is why I turn to you. It takes caring people like you to help people in need: the forsaken, hungry, and suffering.

Will you be the one to provide food, clothing, and shelter to people in desperate need?

These are God's children. They need our help. I pray that knowing how much your generous gift will touch their hearts and lift their spirits will be your reward.

Thank you for reading my letter … and for any gift you can spare.

Please pray for the people we serve.

Sincerely,

Guy Adams

Guy Adams
President

P.S. I have enclosed a handy notepad as a gift for you. May we never take any item of food for granted. Please select the mini "meal ticket" that represents the gift of your choice and return it with your donation in the provided envelope. **Thank you again!**

216-08A-SLTF

81

YOUR 2020 GIVING STATEMENT

Thank you so much for giving generously to the work of Catholic Charities of Acadiana in 2020. Because of your help, we were able to extend the mercy of Christ to so many who were experiencing homelessness, hunger and poverty in our community.

8,596
Supplemental food bags provided through the Seven Day Staples Project

183,000+
Meals provided through St. Joseph Diner, in partnership with Second Harvest Food Bank

472
Individuals assisted in homelessness prevention

500+
Homes touched in response to Hurricanes Laura and Delta

1,076+
Requests for immediate or long-term disaster recovery assistance

153
Men, women, children and veterans provided safe shelter

In addition to the worldwide COVID-19 pandemic, we are responding to two major hurricanes that made landfall roughly 13 miles apart and within a span of six weeks. For so many in our area, this is far too much for them to bear. We respond on behalf of those who support and pray for us, responding to those who cannot rebound on their own and to those who suffer under the burden of multiple disasters. **We cannot do this work alone; it is only with the help of community partners like you that we are able to continue providing essential services to those who are at risk in our community.** Please know how grateful we are for your generosity toward those that we serve

Thank you for continuing to help Catholic Charities of Acadiana care for the sacred gift of all human life, especially the most vulnerable.

Ben Broussard
Chief Communications Officer
Catholic Charities of Acadiana

ben@catholiccharitiesacadiana.org
(337) 235-4972 x1208

Catholic Charities of Acadiana

Catholic Charities of Acadiana
P.O. Box 3177
Lafayette, LA 70502
catholiccharitiesacadiana.org

Operation VetCare

A Project of the
Enlisted Association of the National Guard of the United States

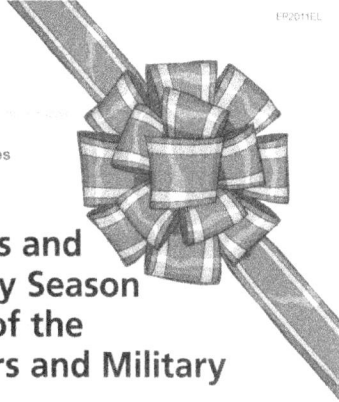

The enclosed address labels and gift tags are a small Holiday Season *"THANK YOU!"* on behalf of the Wounded Veterans, Soldiers and Military families we serve...

Dear Friend,

This holiday season, will you help me bring hope to wounded soldiers and military families who are struggling to overcome injuries and difficulties suffered in the service of our nation?

A few $10 Holiday Grocery Cards, like the ones I enclosed, can help deserving families at this time of year. A visit from members of the National Guard brings relief and hope to a hospitalized veteran or a military family struggling to recover from wounds, tragedy, fire, or flood.

Will you make a holiday sponsorship gift today and help us bring relief and support to those who are striving to recover from disaster or tragedy, or struggling with a service-related injury?

A gift of $10, $20 or $15 can make a difference, and people tell me it's a wonderful way to remember those who served during the holiday season – the perfect gift.

With help from kind friends we can provide year-round assistance

(Over, please)

to members of the Armed Forces and their families when they request it — they are often desperate and facing financial, emotional and physical challenges as a result of the service they are giving to our country.

You can imagine the relief a military family facing hardship feels when we are able to help pay for groceries during the holiday season...

And I'm sure you can imagine the gratitude when a group of strong young guardsmen say "Good morning, ma'am, we are here to fix the roof..."

But there's something more important: When volunteers from the local National Guard show up with a gift, make a home repair, mow the grass, or simply stay and chat, they send a signal that Americans care about members of the armed forces who are struggling.

The year-round assistance we provide is only possible because Operation VetCare receives help from concerned friends like you — we are 100% reliant on contributions and receive NO GOVERNMENT FUNDS.

As the holidays approach, could you find it in your heart to make a holiday gift of $15, $10, $20 or more and help us provide grocery cards, assistance in rebuilding homes, emergency fuel, children's clothing or whatever assistance will make the most difference — and continue providing the other forms of assistance we offer?

Sincerely,

Sgt. Maj. Frank Yoakum, U.S. Army Ret.
Executive Director

P.S.   The labels I enclosed are yours to keep — a small thank you on behalf of a soldier. Will you help me keep up with the requests we receive? If you possibly can, will you make a special **Holiday Season Sponsorship Gift** today?

P.P.S. Especially this year, we offer thanks and support to all the National Guardsmen and their families for all they do to serve our communities.

IIVFW
VETERANS OF FOREIGN WARS.

KN6763

Office of the Adjutant General   www.vfw.org/HelpVeterans | vfwfundraising@vfw.org

November, 2020

Dear Clancy Ratliff,

When we began sending out these free special edition VFW Totes, gifts and check for $2.50, people said we were crazy!

"You can't do it — the VFW will go broke!" many doubters said. "People will use their totes and cash the check, but you'll never hear from them again."

But it didn't turn out that way at all. In fact, thousands of people like you have chosen to help us serve our nation's veterans — many seriously disabled. I'm counting on you to keep helping us prove the doubters wrong ...

But first, what do you see in your mind when you read those words: ***seriously disabled?***

Do you picture a young man or woman in a wheelchair like the one shown here? Maybe you see a veteran with amputated limbs ... a hero with a horribly burned face ... or a veteran who is without speech, lying helpless in a hospital bed.

But what about those veterans who suffer in silence — those who carry the invisible wounds of war?

To pass them on the street you would never know they're terrorized night and day by the horror of Post-Traumatic Stress (PTS). You wouldn't be able to tell they might never hold a job again. You can't "see" the nightmares or sleeplessness.

And you wouldn't know the pain and confusion they feel from Traumatic Brain Injury (TBI).

But that doesn't mean those injuries aren't there.

The truth: more than 413,800 military veterans have experienced a TBI ... many of them in Iraq and Afghanistan. Even more young veterans now suffer from crippling mental illnesses like PTS.

For more than 121 years — since 1899 — the VFW has been there for veterans who need help getting the justice they deserve. We are there for veterans of every generation, of every war, who might otherwise just fall through the cracks. The VFW is on the front line in the fight for education, jobs, health care and justice FOR VETERANS ... because **EVERYTHING WE DO, WE DO FOR VETERANS.**™

(over, please)

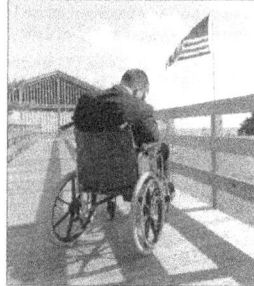

NO ONE DOES MORE FOR VETERANS.

National Headquarters | 406 West 34th Street | Kansas City, MO 64111 | 833.VFW.GIVE (833.839.4483)

50722LRC-5-A

85

We also believe in honoring the service of all veterans by displaying the United States flag, especially on patriotic holidays. And we hope you do, too.

"Old Glory" is still the greatest symbol of our national unity. Displaying the United States flag proudly shows your support for our American values and for those who fought, and are still fighting, to defend them.

When these wounded young veterans who have come home from Iraq and Afghanistan see the flag displayed, it will mean a lot to them. I say that as a veteran myself — and someone who knows just how much the simple appreciation of fellow Americans really means.

You can visit **heroes.vfw.org/Flag** and print a free flag poster for you to display at your home.

But the best way to show you care for our veterans is by sending your tax-deductible gift to the VFW today.

America's defenders rely on the VFW. **NO ONE DOES MORE FOR VETERANS.**

We need patriotic citizens like you to step up to help these veterans whose lives are forever changed by war. Your donation will support critical VFW programs that give veterans a voice on Capitol Hill, help them fight for their hard-earned VA benefits and offer assistance applying for financial relief to cover rent, food or other essentials.

And for those heroes who don't come back, we work to make sure their spouses and children receive the survivor benefits they need and deserve.

If you know of a veteran or family member who could use our help, please tell them to visit our website at vfw.org. We want to make sure that no one who is suffering and needs our assistance is overlooked. You don't have to be a VFW member to receive our help.

I know you care. But it's important that you care enough to take action. The thousands of wounded veterans who have returned from Iraq and Afghanistan can't wait.

I believe that you're the type of American who, when called upon to do the right thing, will come through every time. Please help the VFW do right by those who need our help after serving our country so bravely.

Thank you and God Bless America.

FOR VETERANS,

Kevin C. Jones
Adjutant General

P.S. The enclosed special edition VFW Totes and other gifts, designed exclusively for patriotic supporters of the VFW like you, are yours to keep. Please let me know you received them by returning the Program Participation Form. And please return the $2.50 check along with your special gift to help us reach even more veterans who need the VFW.

P.P.S. With your gift of $15 (or more) by the date on the Program Participation Form, you'll receive your FREE Shopping Bags! See enclosed insert for more details.

90722LRC3-B

From the desk of
MICHAEL S. LINNINGTON

Dear Friend,

For Edil and his family, things were getting desperate. *"My family and I were struggling to pay the oil delivery, trash, groceries, and my electric bill as well."*

But thanks to friends like you, Wounded Warrior Project® (WWP) came through for them with help when they needed it most.

Edil is one of more than 11,000 veterans who received direct financial help from WWP to get through the COVID-19 pandemic. In less than three weeks, we distributed over $11 million in emergency assistance!

Many of these heroes wrote to tell us the grants came just in time. Edil said:

> *"Please know that the Covid-19 grant money received did go to our family, and we are eternally grateful. I thank WWP's entire staff, donors, supporters, and sponsors who made this possible. God bless you all!"*

I can't imagine where our nation would be without heroes who serve to defend our freedom. We are honored to assist our wounded warriors when they need help. With your support, we will continue to be there for them with life-changing programs and services to help them overcome their injuries, get through tough times, and thrive again. Thank you.

To honor and empower,

Michael S. Linnington
Lieutenant General, U.S. Army, Retired
Chief Executive Officer, Wounded Warrior Project

"He who wears the Purple Heart has given of his blood in the defense of his homeland and shall forever be revered by his fellow countrymen."

– GEORGE WASHINGTON

WOUNDED WARRIOR PROJECT°

Dear Caring Friend,

It was his third deployment, this time to Afghanistan, when an improvised explosive device (IED) detonated, leaving Anthony Villarreal's body badly burned.

Unimaginable agony ... third-degree burns over 70 percent of his body ... more than 70 painful surgeries — this is what awaited Anthony upon his return from service.

After he finally awoke from months in a coma, Anthony faced a long and excruciating recovery that continues even today.

Heroes like Anthony can overcome their injuries and succeed again. As a veteran who served for more than 30 years, I've seen them triumph time and time again! *But sometimes even the strongest heroes need help.*

Purple Heart recipient Anthony Villarreal was severely injured while serving in Afghanistan.

That's where Wounded Warrior Project® (WWP) comes in. Since 2003, we've been tireless advocates for our nation's finest, improving the lives of over a million warriors and their families!

Warriors never pay a penny for our programs — because they paid their dues on the battlefield. Our free programs and services in mental health, career counseling, and long-term rehabilitative care change lives.

Because I believe you care about our nation's wounded warriors, I hope you'll use the enclosed **notepad, bookmarks, and set of personalized address labels** to show your support.

I also hope Anthony's story will inspire you to give back to the service-injured veterans who gave so much for you and me.

Will you please send your special gift of $10, $15, or $25 to WWP today to help more injured veterans like Anthony?

Just think of the tragic injuries our heroic servicemen and women suffer from as they fight for our freedom. *Traumatic brain injuries (TBIs) ... amputations of their arms and legs ... burns covering their bodies and scarring their faces ... nerve*

(over, please)

damage that puts them in wheelchairs for life.

They gave their all for our country — for you and for me.

That's why we _must_ be there for them now. **And you can help!** With your support, WWP is transforming the way America's injured veterans are empowered, employed, and engaged in our communities.

Transitioning from military to civilian life is a journey, and that journey is different for every veteran. Those who have sustained severe injuries face the greatest challenges of all.

That's why WWP offers a wide range of free programs and services to support our heroes, no matter what their journey looks like.

We're committed to helping injured veterans achieve their highest ambitions. And your support makes that possible.

As soon as you send your gift, your kindness will start reaching our injured heroes in hospitals overseas, even before they return to the United States for more surgeries, care, and rehabilitation. You'll assist them in rebuilding their lives.

I urge you to go to our website, **woundedwarriorproject.org**, to learn more about the veterans and families you'll be helping.

You'll find lots of ways to participate in our mission and help spread the word about the needs of our brave warriors who sacrificed so much for our freedoms.

But the best way for you to help our heroes right now is by providing your financial support.

Anthony has experienced the impact of WWP programs firsthand. Today, he has a job, a loving family, and a positive outlook. And he's putting his knowledge and experience to work to help other heroes do the same!

Your gift of $10, $25, or maybe even $50 will change the future for an injured veteran. So please be as generous as you possibly can. Thank you for joining Anthony and me in this great cause today!

Saluting your kindness,

Michael S. Linnington
Lieutenant General, U.S. Army, Retired
Chief Executive Officer, Wounded Warrior Project

P.S. *Warriors never pay a penny for our programs — because they paid their dues on the battlefield. With your support, our free services in mental health, career counseling, and long-term rehabilitative care change lives.*

P.P.S. **Please also take a moment now to sign and return the enclosed thank-you card along with your best gift today. I'll make sure your message is delivered to a veteran whose spirits need a lift.**

C2010-11_AT_AA

89

BOOK REVIEWS

Scholarship as a Source of Innovation/Inspiration

Curt Porter

Our call for book reviews this year emphasized the intellectual work involved in the everyday lives of teacher-scholars. We were seeking out personal accounts of how scholarship becomes (or fails to become) relevant in the material, institutional, and ideological realities staring us in the face each time we walk into a classroom. Looking back on roughly ten years since I accepted a tenure track position at a large public university, it's clear that the challenges of my workplace continue to evolve and continue to surprise me. I often find myself in need of new sources of innovation and inspiration. Institutional constraints chalked up to budgetary 'realities' and demands for documented (*read: statistical*) results are fixtures in my work as a teacher. Meanwhile, students come to my first-year writing courses with aspirations, skills, needs, and even language that I sometimes struggle to understand. In this setting, constant innovation can seem like a basic survival skill necessary just to maintain a sense of meaning and professional purpose.

The two reviews included in this issue respond to uncertainties familiar to anyone who strives to innovate in diverse teaching/learning environments. They illustrate a familiar contrast in the ways that scholarship can impact college writing instruction. In our first review, Iwona emphasizes the concept of *becoming* with its potential to foster a social justice curriculum and to resist "business-like" sensibilities in educational settings. We get a sense of the value and the hope that comes with encountering new conceptual toolkits or radical shifts in philosophical perspective. The second review invokes Willa's passion for gaming and explains how the concept of *gamification* can extend to unexpected aspects of a writing course. She demonstrates that sometimes practical or technological 'know-how' is the key to bringing big ideas to life. Together, these pieces offer a reminder that we can turn to scholarly work for different kinds of support, as innovation and inspiration can hit suddenly through new ways of thinking, just as they can be cultivated through a close examination of our daily teaching plans and practices.

Strom, Kathryn J. and Adrian D. Martin. *Becoming-Teacher: A Rhizomatic Look at First-Year Teaching.* Sense Publishers, 2017, 138 pages.

Iwona Ionescu

Rider University

Just before opening the door to the classroom (I teach composition at a four-year college), I pause for a moment. My heart is beating faster—partly because of the four flights of stairs I have just climbed, partly because of the joy of teaching, and partly because of the unknown before me. I have taught writing for twelve years, and yet, I have never taught this particular class to this particular group of students at this particular time and place. I am a composition instructor, and at the same time, I am not the instructor I was a semester ago or even yesterday. I am constantly *becoming* an instructor for the unique set of circumstances I find myself in every semester and every day.

Becoming is one of the central concepts of the rhizomatic approach of Gilles Deleuze and Felix Guattari (1987). It means constantly creating new versions of oneself; in Kathryn J. Strom and Adrian D. Martin's words, it is, "a non-normative ontology corresponding to a dynamic, constantly changing reality" (113). The rhizomatic approach has encouraged me to make peace with the messiness of teaching and learning, and even to find beauty and new possibilities in that messiness. Strom and Martin have given an excellent guide not only to view teaching through a rhizomatic lens but also to make it a tool for enacting social justice. Advocating for social justice, the authors challenge the positivist and neoliberal paradigm that has pervaded education. Several years after the publication of this work, not much has changed in the educational system, and the business-like models are still permeating it. In recent years, scholars have continued their call for social justice in education (e.g., Adams et al., 2016; Parker, 2022; Rice-Boothe, 2023; Smagorinsky, 2024; Venet, 2024), which makes *Becoming-Teacher* particularly relevant today.

By teaching with rhizomatics in mind, teachers create a social justice environment that is at odds with hierarchies and binary logic, characteristic of the traditional, transactional educational paradigms. In the traditional paradigm, engaged/disengaged students are, according to Strom and Martin, "intellectually ranked and segregated" (12) and teachers, who transmit knowledge to students, are perceived as the main factor contributing to student learning. This view disregards important variables influencing learning processes, such as educational institutions and students' socioeconomic status or access to advanced courses. Teachers need to recognize these variables and adapt to the needs of the students. Strom and Martin emphasize constructivist approaches to education, in line with the philosophies of John Dewey, Lev Vygotsky, or Paulo Freire, and argue that it is unrealistic to expect teachers to engage in the same practices every time, as these practices need to be adjusted to specific students and contexts.

This has implications for teacher training. Strom and Martin argue that teacher preparation should include more fieldwork, where future teachers can be exposed to different context-specific situations, and where they can "negotiate their preservice learning with all the actors, elements, and conditions in their new setting" (117). The authors cite research studies that found novice teachers having difficulty transferring the knowledge they gained in their coursework to real classrooms. The authors also provide empirical data through three case studies of novice teachers for whom coursework was just one learning element and who continued to learn their profession on the job. Therefore, extending the period when preservice teachers engage in fieldwork where they can practice co-constructed teaching would diminish the gap between theory and practice. Lastly, those who teach preservice teachers should themselves model co-constructed teaching. As a practical guide, Strom and Martin offer a chart of "rhizomatic shifts in thinking" (113), with a list of characteristics of linear thinking juxtaposed to characteristics of rhizomatic thinking.

Once in the classroom (and outside of it, too, when I meet with my students or plan my classes) I try to practice those rhizomatic shifts in thinking. For example, over time, I have learned that it is unrealistic to expect all my students to process the material at the same pace and to the same extent. Students may not grasp immediately what we do in class; it may take them some time, but this is absolutely fine. I, the instructor, do not have full control over how and when each student will master new knowledge or skills. At any given point, each of my students is at their unique level of skill development, engagement, or maturity. Students should not be penalized for not learning the material I selected within the timeframe that I imposed on them. As an instructor then, I try to guide each student through—and normalize and celebrate students' unique stages of their learning—their unique *becomings*.

Becoming also applies to the process of everchanging teacher identities. The authors illustrate this through three case studies of high school science teachers who are constantly evolving, creating multiple identities, oftentimes at odds with one another. The elements responsible for the multiple identities (e.g., students, colleagues, classrooms, textbooks, or computers) form *teaching-assemblages* (41). For example, one of the teachers, Mauro, taught two different classes, each with very different assemblages of student backgrounds and attitudes, class climate, relationships between students, Mauro's own confidence and knowledge of the subject matter, experience teaching the course, and rapport with the students. Consequently, in each of these classes, Mauro *became* a different teacher, employing very different, often opposing strategies and approaches. While in one class he empowered students to own their learning and feel liberated to co-construct knowledge, in the other one, he assumed a more authoritative role, and to ensure his students' learning, he employed strategies that challenged some of his core beliefs.

Taking a peek into the lived experiences of the teachers who shift between their multiple identities in their daily work has made me rethink my own identity as a composition instructor. We educators may feel the need to define ourselves or other educators in clear categories: authoritarian vs. student-centered, strict vs. lenient. In response to that expectation, I portray myself as a compassionate instructor, who promotes collaborative learning and who seeks connection with her students. However, the rhizomatic approach invites me to reveal a more complex and more honest presentation of myself. While I have created comfortable learning environments, in which I strive to be inclusive and accommodating for my students, I have not always succeeded in creating enough space for collaboration, and depending on the types of colleges where I taught as well as the students' backgrounds and experiences, it has not always been easy for me to connect with every student. I have also often fallen back on creating a linear progression of my characteristics (e.g., from less confident to more confident, or from less knowledgeable to more knowledgeable). Yet the process of *becoming* is not linear and not always predictable. I have had better and worse semesters, as I constantly reinvent myself and adapt to new variables in the classroom and outside-of-class factors that affect me as a person and a professional.

Becoming-Teacher provides a unique angle for approaching teaching and enacting social justice through recognizing the multiplicity of factors responsible for one's learning and treating each student as a respected individual. Rhizomatics can be counted among the "[e]quitable, progressive, and social justice pedagogies" and as such it has "the potential to reshuffle the ... norms of schooling" (78). The book inspires educators to reflect on their practices, regardless of the subject matter or level. The rhizomatic perspective may serve as a practical tool to help create a more equitable environment where learning and identity are understood as ever-changing processes.

Works Cited

Adams, M., Bell, L. A., Goodman, D., & Joshi, K. Y., editors. *Teaching for Diversity and Social Justice.* 3rd ed., Routledge, 2016.

Deleuze, Gilles, and Félix Guattari. *A Thousand Plateaus: Capitalism and Schizophrenia.* Translated by Brian Massumi, University of Minnesota Press, 1987.

Parker, K. N. *Literacy Is Liberation: Working Toward Justice through Culturally Relevant Teaching.* ASCD, 2022.

Rice-Boothe, M. *Leading within Systems of Inequity in Education: A Liberation Guide for Leaders of Color.* ASCD, 2023.

Smagorinsky, P. "Emotions, Empathy and Social Justice Education." *English Teaching: Practice & Critique*, vol. 23 no. 3, 2024, pp. 332–51.

Venet, A. S. *Becoming an Everyday Changemaker: Healing and Justice at School.* Taylor & Francis, 2024.

Adare-Tasiwoopa ápi, Sierra and Nathan K. Silva. *Gamification in Higher Education: A How-to Instructional Guide.* Routledge, 2024, 252 pages.

Willa Black
Indiana University of Pennsylvania

As an avid gamer who is looking to add more gamification into my composition courses, I was immediately intrigued by Adare-Tasiwoopa ápi and Silva's practical focus on gamification in classrooms. While I had explored a lot of the theory on assessments of gamification, I'd hoped that the book would point me in the direction of some techniques and examples that I could quickly implement into my own classrooms. The book delivers on that, and even offers some activities that I would never have interpreted as being "gamified." With each chapter and section focusing on different levels of gamification (a small game such as *Jeopardy*, a large activity/module like a mock trial, or an entire gamified course), the organization of the book was ideal for when I needed a classroom activity or when I wanted to plan out future potential courses or modules. This book is also very timely, as gamification (digital or otherwise) appears to be gaining steam in education (Oliveira et al., 2023; Zeybek & Saygi, 2024).

The book offers an overall introduction followed by four sections, each discussing various levels of gamification in a course such as a single activity, a large assignment, a unit, and an entire course. The authors begin by defining gamification and justifying its use in higher education. They consider a range of perspectives on gamification, explaining various terms associated with it and the activities discussed in the book. They draw on scholars such as Pelling (2011), who was the first to define gamification, albeit in a very technologically-centered way, in the early 2000's and Deterding et al. (2011), who emphasized the importance of "serious" games for learning. They then effectively explain why gamification belongs in higher education where play and games "tend to be a sticking point for many educators" (27). The section ends with a clear and practical list of dos and don'ts. This section could be crucial to help instructors make a case for gamification in their courses to administrators and evaluation committees, particularly for temporary instructors, teaching assistants, or not-yet-tenured faculty who are less established or secure in their current positions.

Section II offers practical instructions and examples with a focus on case studies and role playing as gamification. For example, Chapter 4 details a case study of a fictional woman created for the course named Mercy used to engage students in a Women's and Gender Studies course. The authors provide the entire series of questions/story related to the main character; they also explain what students should learn from this activity and how similar cases could be used. This transitions nicely into Chapter 5's strong focus on role-playing and potential ways to leverage it to bring various forms of representation into the classroom. The section ends by discussing a mock trial, arguably the most complicated and intense activity of the section, and a "whodunit" activity. This section is ideal for instructors who not only want to jump straight into gamification but also have the confidence and experience to plan for such a large portion of their course.

Section III discusses completely gamified courses in its three chapters. In many ways, this is the strongest section of the book. The authors clearly and concisely explain each major project of the courses represented, which come from the fields of biology, composition/English, American Studies, and nursing. Each separate system of points and badges students could receive in each course is clearly explained, contextualized, and justified using classroom experiences. For example, in Chapter 8, the authors describe a fully gamified biology course in which students take on the role of cadets on a colony on Mars. Their assignments come in the form of "missions" from their instructor, the "base commander." Their successes lead to them gaining access to new modules and "star points" which could be exchanged for various assets like study guides or practice tests. Despite how daunting a completely gamified course like this is to think about, each chapter is presented in such a way that it makes the prospect seem doable, even to someone who has only used review games in class.

Section IV introduces and, occasionally, reframes the simplest forms of gamification. Chapter 12 describes various forms of tabletop games, which can be particularly useful for a quick activity to bring into the classroom. Chapters 13 and 14 address games that were frequently referenced as part of the gamified courses, while Chapter 15 goes into recognizable games that many students will know, such as *Jeopardy*. The book concludes with a short summary of a few key points and concepts to keep in mind when implementing gamification, some words of encouragement, and a great "end game" pun. This "toolbox" section was what I was originally anticipating when I began this book, and it's one of the reasons that it will remain on my (electronic) bookshelf for future classes.

The greatest strengths of this book are its practicality as well as its emphasis on what didn't work in their "lessons learned" section at the end of most chapters. Adare-Tasiwoopa ápi's story of her multiple attempts and failures to engage her students in the mock trial, particularly how the side that lost the trial "took out their frustrations with losing on their end of the semester course evaluations" (76) offers insight into course development. Many instructors, myself included, may worry about how students would react to "losing" in a gamified course or module and how that could affect the overall success of the course. These "lessons-learned" descriptions effectively warn readers of potential pitfalls while also offering potential solutions.

The main drawback with the book is that many of the technical aspects are tailored for the learning management system Canvas, and the authors offered only limited advice on how to use other systems or how to incorporate their gamification examples into classrooms/courses with limited access to technology. This is particularly important for instructors in areas with limited internet access or whose students have limited access to technology. In addition, many of the gamified courses discussed in the book were asynchronous, and adding in more advice for other LMSs and technology-free versions would help this book be useful to a wider range of instructors and institutions.

In short, this book is ideal for instructors who are relatively new to gamification or who feel uncomfortable with their ability to incorporate it into their classes. It offers clear, useful, detailed examples for a wide range of courses, subjects, and levels, and the explanations can be very helpful for instructors, provided they use Canvas as their LMS. This book does a good job of completing its purpose: offering practical ways to help instructors add more gamification techniques to their repertoire as these practices gain popularity in education. I, for one, am looking forward to adding systems like "star points" and badges into future courses to further engage and motivate my students.

Works Cited

Oliveira, W., J Hamari, L. Shi, A. M. Toda, L. Rodrigues, P. T. Palomino, and S. Isotani. "Tailored Gamification in Education: A Literature Review and Future Agenda." *Education and Information Technologies,* vol. 28, 2023, pp. 373-406. https://doi.org/10.1007/s10639-022-11122-4

Zeybek, N. and E. Saybi. "Gamification in Education: Why, Where, When, and How? —A Systematic Review. *Games and Culture,* vol. 19, no. 2, 2024, pp. 237-264.

Contributors to *JAEPL*, Vol. 29

Abdullah-Al-Musayeb is a graduate student in the English Department at the University of Louisiana at Lafayette. His research focuses on multimodal composition and the teaching of writing. abdullah-al-.musayeb1@louisiana.edu

Miriam Atkin is a writer whose work concerns the possibilities of poetry in conversation with avant-garde film, music, and dance. She has written three chapbooks: *Fours* (Wendy's Subway), *Lineaments* (Belladonna), and *Inclination Drawing* (Beautiful Days Press). She teaches writing at Bard College and the Otisville Correctional Facility. miriam.atkin@gmail.com

Joshua Barsczewski is Assistant Professor of English Literature and Writing, Writing Program Director, and Writing Center Director at Muhlenberg College. He has published in *Composition Forum*, *Peitho*, and is the co-editor of a forthcoming collection on academic labor, tentatively titled *Adequate: Writing New Logics of Success in Rhetoric and Composition*. joshuabarsczewski@muhlenberg.edu

Willa Black is a Ph.D. Candidate in the Composition and Applied Linguistics program at Indiana University of Pennsylvania as well as the Associate Director of the Kathleen Jones White Writing Center. An avid gamer and language learning enthusiast, her research interests are digital game-based language learning, language learner identity, and writing center administration. willa.swift.black@gmail.com

Iwona Ionescu is a PhD Candidate in Composition and Applied Linguistics at Indiana University of Pennsylvania. She coordinates composition tutoring and teaches first year-composition (FYC) at Rider University. She has worked as an English as a Second Language instructor and professional writing tutor. Iwona's interests include FYC pedagogies, L2 writers, and students' academic writing voices. iionescu@rider.edu

Barja Islam is a Graduate Teaching Assistant, currently pursuing her second Master's degree in English (Literature) at the University of Louisiana at Lafayette. She completed her undergraduate and Master's degrees from the University of Rajshahi, Bangladesh. Her research interests include South Asian Literature, Diasporic Literature, ELT and AI-Based Learning. She has published a paper titled "Teachers' Perceptions and Hesitancy: Integrating ChatGPT as a Tool in English Language Learning" in the *International Journal of Studies in Education and Science*. barja.islam1@louisiana.edu

Florianne Jimenez is Assistant Professor of English at the University of New Hampshire. She has published in *Journal for the History of Rhetoric* and *Journal of Asian American Studies*. She is at work on a monograph on writing, race, and American colonial rule in early 20th century Philippines. Florianne.Jimenez@unh.edu

Jonathan M. Marine is a writing teacher and PhD Candidate in the Writing and Rhetoric program at George Mason University where he also Co-Directs the Northern Virginia Writing Project. His research interests include writing engagement, content analysis, longitudinal writing development, graffiti rhetorics, and the pedagogy and theory of James Moffett. jonathanmmarine@gmail.com

Mithila Mumtaz is a PhD student in English with a concentration in Literature at the University of Louisiana at Lafayette, where she also serves as a Graduate Teaching Assistant. Her academic interests span diverse realms, including American literature, feminist theory, rhetorical analysis, emerging literary discourses, film, and media. She can be reached at mithila.mumtaz1@louisiana.edu.

Dr. Ruth Nathan is a former elementary and middle school teacher, school-based language and literacy consultant, and Visiting Scholar at the University of California, Berkeley. She received her doctorate in reading from Oakland University and has published widely on reading, literacy, and the language arts including a chapter in the 2011 edition of the *Handbook of Reading Research*. ruthienathan@comcast.net.

Rosol Otear is a PhD student in Linguistics at the University of Louisiana at Lafayette and has Masters degrees in TESOL and Applied Linguistics. With a focus on improving second and foreign language learning, she is currently working on developing accessible and comprehensible teaching materials for language learners to enhance their learning experience. Rosol.otear1@louisiana.edu

Clancy Ratliff is Professor of English and Associate Dean of the College of Liberal Arts at the University of Louisiana at Lafayette. Her interests are feminist rhetorics, composition pedagogy, environmental rhetorics, and concepts of authorship and plagiarism. Her research has been published in *Pedagogy*; *Teaching English in the Two-Year College*; *Kairos: A Journal of Rhetoric, Technology, and Pedagogy*; *Women's Studies Quarterly*, and other journals and edited collections. She is involved with several community advocacy organizations, including Sierra Club Delta Chapter, Citizens' Climate Lobby, and the Acadiana Regional Coalition on Homelessness and Housing (ARCH). clancy.ratliff@louisiana.edu

Simon Richard is a senior at the University of Louisiana at Lafayette. He is pursuing a bachelor's degree in General Studies with a concentration in Humanities. He has had a lifelong passion for education and wisdom and hopes to spread that in his writing. He also hopes to put his gifts to use in a career in civil service. simon.richard1@louisiana.edu

Noah Smith is a professional writer specializing in copywriting and editing. He obtained his BA in English from the University of Louisiana at Lafayette in Professional Writing. Currently, he is pursuing his Master's in English focusing in Professional Writing. As a graduate assistant for the Center for Louisiana Studies at the university, he assists the editorial department in editing and reviewing manuscripts (fiction and nonfiction) focused on Louisiana history and heritage. noah.smith1@louisiana.edu

Nuzhat Tarannum is an English Language Instructor and MA student in the TESOL program at the University of Louisiana at Lafayette. Her research interests include writing Sociolinguistics, Language Variation, Political Rhetoric, Second Language Acquisition, critiquing narratives, pedagogy practices, and content analysis. nuzhat.tarannum1@louisiana.edu

Allyssa Veney completed her Bachelor of Arts at Louisiana State University. She is currently completing her Masters and Doctorate in English at the University of Louisiana at Lafayette. Her areas of interest include literary studies, creative writing, performing arts, classics, education, and human development. allyssa.veney1@louisiana.edu

ANNOUNCEMENT

The Giving and the Receiving: Spiritual Traditions and Teaching

AEPL SUMMER CONFERENCE

June 12–15, 2025

YMCA of the Rockies
Estes Park, CO

See AEPL.ORG

PARLOR PRESS

EQUIPMENT FOR LIVING

Now with Parlor Press!

Studies in Rhetorics and Feminism
New Series Editors: Jessica Enoch and Sharon Yam

Emerging Conversations in the Global Humanities
Series Editor: Victor E. Taylor

New Releases

Writing Proposals and Grants 3e by Richard Johnson-Sheehan and Paul Thompson Hunter

Rhetorics of Evidence: Science – Media – Culture edited by edited by Olaf Kramer and Michael Pelzer

Kenneth Burke's Rhetoric of Identification by Tilly Warnock

The Forever Colony by Victor Villanueva

Keywords in Making edited by Jason Tham

Inclusive Aims: Rhetoric's Role in Reproductive Justice edited by Heather Brook Adams and Nancy Myers

Not Playing Around: Feminist and Queer Rhetorics in Videogames by Rebecca Richards

Design for Composition: Inspiration for Creative Visual and Multimodal Projects by Sohui Lee and Russell Carpenter

MLA Mina Shaughnessy Prize and CCCC Best Book Award 2021!

Creole Composition: Academic Writing and Rhetoric in the Anglophone Caribbean, edited by Vivette Milson-Whyte, Raymond Oenbring, and Brianne Jaquette

Check Out Our Website!

Discounts, blog, open access titles, instant downloads, and more.

www.parlorpress.com

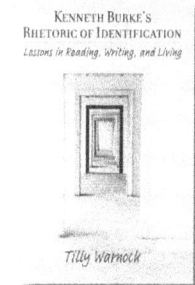